# DEADLY WEEKEND

## A True Story of Obsession and Murder

JOHN DILLMANN

G. P. PUTNAM'S SONS
New York

The author gratefully acknowledges permission from the following sources to quote from material in their control: *The States-Item* and *The Times-Picayune.* Arthur Lemann's closing argument in the John Smith murder trial is reprinted with Mr. Lemann's permission.

G. P. Putnam's Sons
*Publishers Since 1838*
200 Madison Avenue
New York, NY 10016



*Designed by Rhea Braunstein*

Library of Congress Cataloging-in-Publication Data

Dillmann, John.
Deadly weekend : a true story of obsession and murder / John Dillmann.—1st American ed.
p. cm.
ISBN 0-399-13556-1
1. Murder—Louisiana—New Orleans—Investigation—Case studies.
I. Title.
HV6534.N45D547 1991 90-45459 CIP
364.1'523'0976335—dc20

Printed in the United States of America
1 2 3 4 5 6 7 8 9 10

This book is printed on acid-free paper.

# *Acknowledgments*

I want to give special thanks, as always, to my family—Diane, Todd, and Amy.

Thanks also to Fred Dantagnan, my dear friend, with whom I've shared so many adventures.

Thanks to Judy Hoffman; William, Joe, Terri, and John Hoffman; Lea, Ethan, and Micah Lewis; John and Anita Reeves; Leonard and Bess McBrayer; the Blackledges; Joe and Linda Lewandoski; Marty Reisman; Jerry and Jane Shields; Charles and Rudy Ced; Betty Duke; Victoria Cerinich; and Steve Horton.

The book benefited greatly from the inspired editing of Lisa Wager and Edward Olinger.

My gratitude to Dick Price; Kenneth, Stephayne, and Staci Price; Debbie Knoll; Debbie Russell; Betty Woodard; Joe Bradham; Don and Linda Guillot; Buddy Lemann; Joe Meyer; and my parents, John P. Dillmann, Jr., and Beverly Dillmann.

*With love to my grandparents,*
*Gladys McKnight and the late Howard McKnight.*

# •1•

PUTTING our heads together a few minutes into the morning of Tuesday, January 24, 1978, detectives on Homicide's graveyard shift solved the mystery of why we had been assigned—unofficially, of course—to investigate the case.

One man felt "insulted"; two others had bruised egos; but all six of us knew we would do our best, if for no better reason than fear of the man who issued the order—our tough, no-nonsense Chief of Detectives, Henry Morris.

"A *missing person,*" one detective hissed with disgust, thinking about how the mighty had fallen. Other cops chased burglars, shoplifters, speeders, but we pursued the most dangerous game. Our look-out was cop shooters, kidnappers, and killers. The cream of detective work.

"It's because he's a goddamn doctor," another decided, his sense of egalitarianism offended. "Goddamn doctors get better service than the average joe."

"Nah," said Pascal Saladino. "It ain't that."

Saladino was to Homicide what Babe Ruth had been to the 1927 Yankees. He ranked as the best player on the murder squad's roster; no, the best on the entire force. He was that rare piece of work, a detective in more than just name (he is, incidentally, still on the job, with thirty-two years under his belt), absolutely uncanny, possessing a sixth sense for zeroing in on a killer and, more important, *proof* of guilt. Pascal had nominated me for Homicide six years earlier, a signal honor coming from him, and along with everyone else this early morning, my head turned to hear what he had to say.

"Anybody," Saladino lectured, flicking ashes onto the floor from the big, vile cigar he smoked, "could get the same preferential treatment if—that's the key word—*if* the circumstances were the same. None of us have seen a situation quite like this before, that's all."

He was right. On Thursday, January 19, a wealthy St. Petersburg, Florida, anesthesiologist named Mark Sheppard had flown to New Orleans for a weekend vacation. When he failed to show up for scheduled surgery on Monday morning, January 23 (*today* until a few minutes ago), three of his friends became so alarmed that they and a high-dollar private investigator named Dick Price immediately flew to the Crescent City to demand an investigation. Then Price showed an unnerving talent for pushing the right button. He called Chief of Detectives Henry Morris and claimed that only the demise, or more probably the murder, of the ever-reliable and exceedingly punctual Dr. Sheppard could have prevented him from showing up for that scheduled operation.

Chief Morris, an experienced hand, told Price to call the missing-persons unit. But the p.i. didn't discourage so easily. Suspecting correctly that the struggling NOPD missing-persons unit was woefully understaffed—in fact, the "unit" consisted of *one* officer, Gary Himel—Price demanded that some real manpower be assigned to the investigation. In most instances the easily annoyed Morris would have given the private dick an earful and told him to get lost, but the Floridian touched an exposed nerve by saying, "Doctor Sheppard has been murdered. I'm sure of it. And if your people won't do their job and solve the case, I will."

"You see," Saladino said, "it's all about money and pride. Money because the city fathers fear a loss of serious bucks if there's a wave of publicity about how a wealthy tourist can come here to have a good time and end up dead. But as far as the department is concerned, pride's more important. Morris can't tolerate the idea of an outsider solving one of our cases."

I couldn't go home when graveyard ended. I was supposed to testify in a murder trial that day, and the office qualified as good a place as any to wait to be called. I poked my head into Homicide Commander Tom Duffy's office to say hello and pass some time, and he waved me inside.

"What next? What next?" Duffy looked forlorn, a natural enough state for a man with his daily view of the human condition. He sat slumped in his chair facing the never-shrinking pile of reports on his desk. I sat down across from him. "We don't have enough headaches from murders, rapes, and police shootings. Now Henry wants us to take on missing persons, too."

I kept quiet.

"You hear about this shit with the doctor from Florida?" he asked.

"Yeah. It's all over the office."

"This Mark Sheppard is loaded. Serious bucks. No one hears from him for a few days and a search party comes running. We have to work on this one because Henry says so, and we don't even have a body. With our luck, he'll turn up on holiday. A whole lot of hassle and bullshit because this guy's got money, and because we'll look like fools if he is dead and a *goddamn p.i.,* for chrissake, solves the case on our turf."

"How you gonna handle it?"

"I'll have Gary and Hector check it out. It's probably a big flap over nothing."

Maybe so, I thought. Someone missing after a weekend in the French Quarter was not a rarity.

Duffy shuffled his weary frame to the door. "Hector! Gary! In my office!"

George Heath, aka Big Hector, had formerly partnered with George Florane. We kept getting the two Georges mixed up, so we arbitrarily dubbed Heath as Hector. Jovial, likable, a tough old street cop with a receding hairline, Big Hector stood 6′2″, weighed 240 pounds, and now teamed up with Gary Melerine, also 6′2″ and 240. They could have passed for twins, except Melerine had more hair.

"I need you to look into the Sheppard case," Duffy told them.

"Oh, come on," Heath said. "I've got five open homicides, one of them a heater. This is small stuff."

Duffy tried diplomacy. "This 'small stuff' is a problem that's not going to go away till we get some answers."

Though he didn't realize it at the time, Duffy had made the understatement of the year. The Sheppard disappearance would soon explode from a minor annoyance into one of the most difficult and painful cases of my career.

"It's a fucking missing person." Hector held his ground.

The carrot hadn't worked, so Duffy switched to the stick. "I know, Hector," he said. "I know. But Henry wants it done."

Stating this simple fact ended the argument. Even Saladino, with all the slack the department rightly cut him, would have backed down.

"It's probably bullshit," Duffy conceded. "But if it isn't, this Florida p.i. could make us look like dumb butts. Go interview the three friends. They're at the Ursulines Guest House."

"That's where Sheppard was staying," Heath said.

"According to his friends. But who knows? Shit, it could be anything."

"What about the p.i.?" Melerine asked.

"Stay ahead of him. Whatever you do, don't let him into Sheppard's room. If it looks like there's nothing to this, maybe we can short-stop the press conferences I'm sure he intends to call."

Three hours later I was still waiting to be summoned to court when Hector and Melerine returned from the Ursulines Guest House. I asked them for an update.

"You want to work all three shifts, Dillmann?" Big Hector asked, grinning.

"No. I'm just curious. Besides, I understand we're all invited to this party. Be a good guy, Hector, and tell me what you learned."

The Ursulines Guest House, 708 Ursulines Street, a converted residence in the heart of the French Quarter near Jackson Square, was a very exclusive, very expensive hotel. Not advertised in tourist brochures nor bedecked with an ornately lettered shingle or neon tubing, this sedate hostelry sat anonymously on a quiet street. Visitors had to knock to get inside the office, and guests were provided a key to enter privately through a solid iron door that led to a courtyard and from there to the rooms.

After rousing the manager, Heath and Melerine met Sheppard's three friends—Edward White, sixty-three; Del Woodard, fifty-two; and Chris Moore, twenty-five—in the lobby. Ed White and Del Woodard were neighbors of Sheppard's, and Moore managed some of the doctor's extensive property holdings.

First they interviewed Woodard, perhaps Sheppard's

best friend, and he provided a good description of the doctor: age 50, 5′11″, 180 pounds, salt-and-pepper hair, always clean-shaven, a stylish dresser who wore horn-rimmed glasses and had no scars, marks, or other distinguishing features. Woodard emphasized that the doctor was extraordinarily reliable, punctual to a fault, *never* late. "Thank God you've responded," Woodard concluded. "We have a terrible feeling about all this. I know something horrible has happened to him."

"When did Doctor Sheppard arrive in New Orleans?" Heath asked.

"Thursday. The nineteenth. There's something you need to know about Doc. He's head of anesthesiology at St. Anthony's Hospital. It's a very stressful job and he works like a Trojan. Except for occasional trips abroad, long weekends in New Orleans are his main relaxation."

"Why New Orleans?" Melerine asked.

"Why New Orleans?" Woodard seemed surprised. "Look at the history, the cuisine, the ambiance of this city. Doc's been in love with it for years, and has many friends here. He intended to donate an art piece to one of your museums on this trip. A valuable Andrew Jackson bust worth fifty thousand dollars."

"Which museum?"

"I'm sorry, I don't know. I do know he brought the bust with him from St. Petersburg."

"Anything else you can tell us about Doctor Sheppard?" Heath asked. "His social habits. Is he a heavy drinker?"

"Oh, no, though he appreciates fine wine. Doc has one of the best private wine collections I've ever seen. He's a connoisseur, and not just of wine, but of fine food." Woodard hesitated, then smiled. "Oh, yes, and he shoots pool. Can't get enough of the game. He's very good. He's told me many times how much he enjoys playing in New Orleans, where the competition is much tougher, much keener, than in St. Petersburg."

"Could Doctor Sheppard possibly be staying at a friend's house in New Orleans?"

"Positively not. I hate to keep repeating myself, but let me explain. Doc is a very precise, methodical individual. In the eight years he's run anesthesiology, he's *never* missed a scheduled operation. When he travels, he carefully plans his itinerary and personally double-checks the reservations. I'm telling you, we didn't panic by coming here; something is definitely wrong. This absence is totally, absolutely out of character for him. But to answer your question, no, he's not at a friend's place. He rented a room here at the Ursulines Guest House, and this is where he would stay."

"Can you think of any reason at all that he might want to disappear? Get away for a while?"

"The doc? No. Of course not."

Although Heath and Melerine were impressed that Sheppard had friends who would come all the way from Florida out of concern for his welfare, what they had heard so far didn't justify the intervention of Homicide, or even an all-out effort by Ray Himel, the missing-persons officer. Upwards of a million people each year in this country amaze friends and relatives by "pulling a Houdini," and all other police work would halt if the necessary resources were expended searching for them.

Next the detectives talked to Edward White, who along with his wife, Ida, were among the doctor's closest friends. They had traveled abroad with Sheppard, shared his love of good food and fine art.

Heath and Melerine judged that White was a very prominent citizen in St. Petersburg, a man to whom people listened. He told the detectives that Sheppard often played pool in New Orleans at a place called Cigar's, with three people whose names he remembered: Ponce Woods, Larry Cephas, and someone known as "Candy." White knew nothing about the men except their names.

Big Hector and Melerine knew about Cigar's, however, and it struck them as strange that the sophisticated St. Petersburg doctor frequented a dump like this one, a local watering hole for hustlers, pimps, prostitutes, drunks, runaways, ex-cons, junkies, and dope dealers. Located at 132 Exchange Place—not much more than a narrow, dimly lit alley built in horse-and-buggy days that runs a single block between Canal and Iberville—this seedy little dive catered to degenerates, and customers sauntered in and out through an *opening.* There was no door.

Clearly, Edward White didn't know about Cigar's. Could there be a lot more he didn't know about Dr. Mark Sheppard?

Finally they talked with the young and obviously nervous Chris Moore, whom Heath and Melerine had observed pacing the Ursulines lobby in tight circles. Several times he had started to interrupt the interviews, but stopped himself. His manner practically shouted, *Get me alone. I have something you need to hear, but it's for your ears only.*

"Let's step into the courtyard," Melerine suggested. "Some fresh air will do us good."

They indicated Woodard and White should wait for them and walked Moore out into a crisp, blue-sky January morning.

"Chris," Heath said, and stopped to crank himself up. Big Hector wasn't going to fool around. What they had been hearing about this wonderful doctor didn't jibe with Cigar's. "Chris, let's cut through all the crap and get to the bottom of this bullshit. You have to trust us, work with us, tell us everything, if you expect us to find Doctor Sheppard."

Moore stared at his shoes. He began to talk, then stopped himself. Hector shuffled his feet impatiently, glowered. It wasn't an act with him—the unusual nature of the case had so far made it bearable, but he was wasting time on a missing person when he had murders to solve.

"Well," Moore said, "I guess you really need to know. Very few people in St. Petersburg have any idea. You see, Doctor Sheppard is a pillar of St. Pete society. Highly respected, active in charities, a substantial, rock-solid individual. He . . ."

"Spit it out," Big Hector growled.

Moore shook his head slowly, but the detectives could see his mind was racing, calculating whether he should trust them. Heath and Melerine had no compassion. These burly bookends wanted answers.

"Even people at St. Anthony's," Moore said, "*especially* people there, have no inkling of the truth. I really hope this doesn't have to become public knowledge."

"We'll use discretion," Melerine said. Although in appearance just as intimidating as Heath, Melerine *had* to play soft cop when the situation required. Big Hector was all hard cop and couldn't fake anything else.

"I need your assurances," Moore said.

Annoyance darkened Heath's face, but he managed to keep his tone conversational. "We can't promise you confidentiality," he said, "but we'll try."

Moore thought this over, nodded, and then began. "There's a part of Mark Sheppard's life that few people know about: his sexuality. He prefers young black men. Please understand that Doc is a caring, compassionate person who genuinely deserves the admiration our community has given him. He couldn't be more respected at the hospital, and rightly so. But when the stress gets to be unbearable, Doc takes these long weekends, has a good time far away from the pressure. And what better place than New Orleans?"

"What do you mean by that?" Big Hector said, his voice that of an offended Department of Tourism spokesperson.

"Doc can relax here. He has the best of both worlds: the culture of this old city *and* freedom. He didn't have to look over his shoulder here. No one knew him."

Heath didn't like the idea of his hometown serving as a place for living one's fantasies, but he held his tongue. Like all good cops, he knew not to discourage Moore from talking. A detective won't gather information if he shows disapproval of what he hears. The best interrogators can listen to the recounting of the most hideous crimes without batting an eye.

"Anything else you can tell us?" Melerine asked.

"I know Mark loved to eat at John T's. He raved about the food."

And well he should have. In a city world-renowned for good restaurants, John T's ranked among the best. Located at 1000 North Rampart Street on the fringe of the French Quarter, near Basin Street and Louis Armstrong Park, it featured outstanding French Creole dishes. This was no tourist trap; most of its clientele were locals.

"Is it *possible* Doctor Sheppard could be visiting one of his friends?"

"No," Moore said irritably. "You still don't understand why we've come all the way from Florida. No one is more set in his ways than Mark Sheppard. He is a dyed-in-the-wool bachelor, accustomed to living alone and abiding strictly by his schedule. And he had his expensive Andrew Jackson bust to contend with; Mark wouldn't have dragged that around with him. He knew it would be safe here. The Ursulines has air-tight security and can only be entered or left with a key to that heavy iron door. Doc is not reckless.

Just the opposite. He is very, very cautious about everything he does in New Orleans. He would not, I repeat, *would not* spend the night, much less three or four nights, at someone else's place. I am not a worried mother concerned because her teenage daughter is a few hours late. I know Mark Sheppard and I fear something terrible has happened to him. *Now* do you understand?"

"Yes," said Heath, "but it's time for *you* to understand. Doctor Sheppard is a missing person. He's not dead, just missing, as far as we're concerned. And whatever happened to him has already taken place. We normally don't get involved with missing persons, but the department has made an exception. We'll work this case, and you and your friends can help us. But help, Mr. Moore, don't hinder. Don't hold back information."

"I'm not keeping anything from you."

"Will you be in town for a few days?"

"Yes."

"We'll be in touch."

Next Heath and Melerine talked to Ursulines manager Jim Owens, who revealed that Dr. Sheppard, a regular at the guest house, often invited male prostitutes to his room. In fact, Sheppard had brought home a black man who Owens thought was a prostitute on January 19, the first night of his visit.

"What time did they arrive?" Heath asked.

"About 10:00 P.M."

"When did the black man leave?"

"They left together. At about seven-thirty the next morning."

"Sheppard never returned?"

"No. He hasn't been back."

Heath and Melerine inspected Sheppard's room, found the bust of Andrew Jackson, plus, in the closet, sport coats, suits, shirts, slacks, and ties. His wallet on the dresser contained no money, but inside was a driver's license, Visa and American Express credit cards, and a receipt from John T's restaurant dated January 19. A single one-dollar bill and a Norelco electric shaver sat next to the wallet.

Melerine pulled down the covers of the neatly made bed—a maid had changed the sheets—but found no signs of blood or semen on the mattress. In fact, nowhere was there evidence of a struggle; almost surely no murder had taken place here. If indeed a homicide had occurred, they knew that without a crime scene the case wouldn't be solved for a while.

Nothing in that immaculately kept room helped them. Big Hector couldn't understand how the Andrew Jackson bust could be worth fifty thousand dollars, and frankly, when I later saw it, neither could I.

They sealed the room and took the Jackson bust and the contents of Sheppard's wallet with them. Perhaps the picture off his driver's license could be used for a circular, and the credit cards might provide information about other purchases he'd made *after* eating at John T's. Possibly he had returned to the Ursulines Guest House on January 20 without being noticed, though it was doubtful. The room seemed undisturbed since the maid had cleaned it.

Back at the station, I added up what Heath related and figured Dr. Sheppard had either been murdered or abducted. Most of the evidence pointed in one of those directions: the missed operation, the wallet with his credit cards, the valuable bust left unattended. One thing for sure: Whatever his fate, he hadn't met it at the Ursulines.

I supposed he could have staged his own disappearance, leaving behind personal effects to throw off searchers. Odder things had happened, and I could imagine reasons he might want to vanish, but I suspected the answers were simpler.

We knew the doctor associated with young black males, and clearly the Number-One suspect at this moment was the individual with whom he had left the guest house at 7:30 A.M. on January 20. Finding this man—Owens said he had never seen him before—was the top priority.

Lacking were the three most important elements of a murder investigation, if indeed homicide was what we contended with: a body, a crime scene (usually a gold mine of information), and a motive (we had no idea).

Day shift—8:00 A.M. to 4:00 P.M.—ended and jury selection still hadn't been completed. I wondered whether I should return home to Slidell to grab a bite to eat, a hug from my wife Diane, and a few hours of sleep before starting graveyard, or if I should forsake all semblance of normal, rational behavior and pull a round-the-clock.

Now I wish I had gone home.

# •2•

He wore razor-creased dress slacks, a white silk shirt, a waist-length soft leather jacket, and shoes that would have cost me two-weeks salary. He sported a gold nugget ring on one finger, a horseshoe diamond on another, a gold and diamond Rolex watch, and a heavy gold rope chain around his neck. He had no competition in the clothes department from the assorted J.C. Penney-attired homicide detectives who went about their chores in the murder office. When they spotted this spectacularly tanned Floridian, a few eyes gleamed with amusement, while others made their disdain obvious.

*Real* cops, as they think of themselves, want no truck with "gumshoes," private investigators. Real cops risk their lives to arrest murderers, rapists, drug fiends prowling alleys with knives. Gumshoes sneak around seedy motels trying to catch otherwise ordinary citizens in bedroom dalliances, and hold the hands of snotty, spoiled dowagers with white poodles, people who believe the Mafia is out to kill them and demand twenty-four-hour protection. I knew just such a disturbed person and her p.i., who should have been urging psychiatric care instead of cynically indulging her fantasies while running her tab into the stratosphere.

The bottom-line reason real cops hate gumshoes is that they usually stand on opposite sides of the fight. Private investigators work for the enemy, defense attorneys, whose mission in life real cops fervently believe is to open wide the jailhouse doors and unleash on the citizenry every violent scumbag the good guys have swept off the street.

Dick Price had come to the Homicide office this January 24 evening after talking to Woodard, White, and Moore. They'd given him the names of the detectives who had interviewed them, and now he wanted to speak to Heath or Melerine. They were out trying to get a handle on the identity of the individual who spent the night of January 19 with Sheppard, so the desk sergeant sent the private investigator to me. Having decided not to go home, I was trying to catch up on paperwork.

We sat across from each other at the battered gunmetal gray desk I shared with detectives from the other two shifts. My eyes were bloodshot and I needed a shave. Price, forty-four years old to my thirty-one but approximately the same size—5′11″ and 180—looked as if he had just stepped fresh from a shower, manicure, and hairstyling at his health club. He had powerful hands and arms, and appeared to be in peak condition. The big horseshoe diamond on his right hand reflected shafts of light that stabbed my eyes.

"John," he said, raising his voice to be heard above the hubbub of the large open room. "You don't mind my calling you John, do you?"

"Not at all." I couldn't take my eyes off his gem-studded Rolex watch. I later found out it cost just about what I made in a year.

"John, I came here in person hoping we could get started on the right foot. I think I can be of assistance to this investigation. I've worked as a police officer, was elected to the Florida legislature from Pinellas County, and been pro-law enforcement my entire life. I'm only interested in justice, and really want to work *with* you. Anything I can do, just ask."

"Well, Dick, let's begin. Who hired you?"

"Betty Woodard and Joe Bradham. Mrs. Woodard's husband is in New Orleans now. They're probably Doctor Sheppard's closest friends, and Betty is executrix of his estate. Joe Bradham is the lawyer who drew up the doctor's will. I've worked for Joe before."

"He's just missing, and already they're thinking about the will?"

"No. I told you, the Woodards are Sheppard's best friends. They're very worried that something has happened to him."

"Did you know Doctor Sheppard?"

"No. Joe called yesterday morning. He was very alarmed. I caught a plane to New Orleans later in the day."

"You always provide such quick service?" I stalled, wanting to bring the conversation back around to the will.

"If it's an emergency. In this instance, everyone agreed something bad had happened."

"What do you mean by 'everyone'?"

"The Woodards. Joe Bradham. Other of Sheppard's friends. His associates at the hospital. They all swear the doctor is as reliable as the sunrise."

"About this will. Who benefits?"

"That part fascinates you," he answered after a pause.

"Money is a strong motive for murder." I had handled a case where a son killed his own mother hoping to collect an inheritance.

"Frankly," Price said, "I don't know all the beneficiaries of the will. I understand there are quite a few. One of them, since you ask, just happened to be in New Orleans last Friday, the day the doctor disappeared."

He said it so casually I wondered if he were pulling my leg. I thought not. Price radiated sincerity, too much for my style, but I'd already suspected that what you saw with this man was what you got. Despite all the flash and glitter, he seemed guileless.

"Who was that?"

"His name's Ramon Cabrera, also an M.D. His visit had nothing to do with Sheppard's. Neither knew the other was in town."

"And Doctor Cabrera is a beneficiary of the will?"

"I think so. I know he was before."

"Before?"

"Sheppard changed his will two days before he came to New Orleans."

I decided to hold onto that interesting piece of information for a while. "What can you tell me about Doctor Sheppard?" I said.

"He's extremely wealthy. He collects fine art and antique cars."

"Antique cars?"

"Yes. Rolls-Royces manufactured in the twenties and thirties, formerly owned by famous movie stars. One of them belonged to the actress Linda Darnell, and I'm told it's very valuable. I went to Sheppard's mansion with Joe Bradham before I flew here. The place is magnificent, every room filled with antiques, statues, and paintings, and there's a gorgeous outdoor swimming pool."

"Where does his money come from?"

Price looked at me incredulously, his open-book face filled with amazement. He said simply, "Sheppard's an anesthesiologist."

I continued foolishly. "An anesthesiologist puts people to sleep, right?"

*Where have you been?* Price's expression seemed to say. Instead he said, "A big-time anesthesiologist, which Sheppard definitely is, or maybe was, does a lot better than pretty good. He gets paid as much as five thousand dollars for a single operation."

Time to change direction again. "I understand you're going to hold a press conference to publicize the doctor's disappearance."

"That's correct. Bradham is going to offer a ten-thousand-dollar reward for information leading to Doctor Sheppard's whereabouts."

Chief Morris had seen it coming. And the press conference would generate all the nuttiness—psychics, publicity seekers, crazies rushing to confess, politicians, and chamber of commerce types butting in—he strove to avoid.

"That's a lot of money," I said.

"It is," Price agreed. "But Sheppard's got a lot of money."

"How much? In round figures?"

"He's a millionaire."

"One million? Ten?"

"Listen," Price said. "Why don't I buy you dinner? I'm staying at the Marriott, room 1919, and you can reach me there. But tonight let's test the food at the Court of Two Sisters."

We rode in his rented Lincoln Town Car the four miles to the Court of Two Sisters. Synonymous with fine dining in the French Quarter, this restaurant derived its name from two Creole sisters, Emma and Bertha Comors, who served tea and cakes to favorite customers at the notions shop they opened in 1866 on the first floor of their grand residence at 613 Rue Royale.

I thought about Price as we drove. He had suggested dinner when I pressed him about Sheppard's finances (estate?). I suspected he would offer a quid pro quo—tell me something I didn't know in exchange for something he didn't know—and everything else being equal, I intended to accept. Chief Morris wouldn't approve—he envisioned a self-seeking glory hound bent on stealing NOPD's thunder—but I judged this wouldn't drive Price away, and besides, cooperation beat being at loggerheads with the obviously successful p.i.

A tricky situation. I felt that if Price solved the case, more power to him, but it would be a different matter altogether if he cracked it, and took the credit, using *our* information. I didn't think he would pull such a deception, but I could already hear Morris screaming at me, which wouldn't be the worst of this imagined episode. The chief would calm down and say, "Goddamn, Dillmann, what I should do is fire you clowns on Homicide and replace the bunch of you with that private dick Price. Goddamn. Here's a guy who's worth more than a whole unit."

Despite Price's glitzy trinkets, perhaps necessary accouterments for an upscale p.i. image, he had made a favorable initial impression by offering to cooperate. Although this was in his own interest, it could also indicate he didn't aim to upstage anyone. Plus he'd said all the words guaranteed to soothe the ears of a cop: pro-police, pro-law and order, an interest in justice, etc. I felt the decision to take a chance with him was justified, even though the case wasn't exclusively mine. Chief Morris had said every officer in Homicide had a stake in the Sheppard investigation.

This evening a chilly winter breeze had reserved the Two Sisters' popular courtyard for shadows dancing across the old brick walls and around the fountain. Price and I were seated in the Grand Marquis Room, named in honor of Marquis de Vaudreuil, the most colorful of the early (1743–1753) French governors of Louisiana, whose flamboyant life-style helped transform a primitive colonial settlement into the "Paris of America."

After indulging ourselves in Shrimp Toulouse, Oysters

Jambalaya, and Bananas Foster for dessert, I drank coffee and Price sipped a brandy. "Let's get back to Sheppard's money," I said, hoping to catch a reaction. "How much does he have?"

"What do you suppose happened to him?" the p.i. countered. "Do you think he's still alive?"

I groaned inwardly. The cop and ex-cop parrying routine wouldn't get us anywhere. We each sought to gather information without giving any. The unique aspect of New Orleans Homicide working a missing-person case had planted paranoia in my brain. My mind's eye saw the headline in the *Times-Picayune:* "Private Investigator Makes Fool of Police."

"Who knows if he's alive?" I said inanely. "But if he's been murdered, there had to be a motive."

"Have you come up with anything I can relay to my clients?"

Right. The clients who had just bought me an expensive dinner. I grew silent and started to wrestle with my conscience.

*Grab hold of yourself,* I thought. *This isn't a contest between the police and Price where the loser gets his head chopped off.*

I tried to analyze my problem right there, while Price looked on, and it came down to Henry Morris touching the wrong nerve. The Homicide unit considered itself the elite of the New Orleans Police Department. Handling the crime society deemed most serious, our ratio of murders worked to murders solved ranked among the best in the nation. But maybe deep down we didn't really believe in ourselves. Still, if he did succeed while we failed, perhaps we would learn something valuable.

Whatever. All this seems ridiculous now. Knowing as I do the bizarre way the case turned out, it's ironic to think anyone would struggle to take credit.

"Sheppard was last seen Friday morning," I said, answering the question Price had asked five minutes earlier. "At the intersection of Ursulines and Royal. He was going to the French Market for coffee and beignets."

"How do you know this?"

"The hotel manager."

"Was Sheppard alone?"

"No. He was with another man."

"What man?"

"We don't know. We'll find out. Look, Dick, Doctor Sheppard may have been murdered, may have committed suicide, or possibly he was kidnapped and robbed. I guess he could have reasons for arranging his own disappearance. I'd wager that money is involved."

"You're talking about the will?"

"I don't know. I need to see it. I want to learn who the heirs are. I've got to find out how this Doctor Cabrera fits in."

"I'll try to get a copy."

"Yeah," I said dryly. "Do that. Your client is his attorney. It shouldn't be hard."

Everyone in Homicide had brought murderers to ground by studying the cash motive. That was always the first question: cui bono, who gains? Watergate's Deep Throat had advised Bob Woodward, "Look to the money," a recommendation generally applicable in homicide investigations. Sheppard had just revised his will, and usually an individual informed his beneficiaries. The clue to his disappearance might have nothing to do with New Orleans.

"Did Sheppard arrive at the French Market?" Price asked.

"Not yet," I said.

"What direction do we go?" Price said in a friendly tone.

We? I knew this had been coming and was prepared for

it. "Sheppard," I said, "spent Thursday night at the guest house with a young black male."

Price looked at me, his smile evaporated. I returned his gaze benignly.

"A black *guy?*"

I didn't change expression.

Price whistled. "Jesus Christ. I had it in the back of my head that he might be gay, but Jesus *Kee*rist."

I didn't say a word. I wanted him to feel grateful for the information, specifically to feel he owed me a copy of that will.

"My God, John." He laughed heartily. "This is a bombshell. Talk about someone being deep in the closet! A lot of important people in St. Petersburg are in for a big shock."

"If they find out."

"Yeah. *If.*" Price sipped his brandy and twisted the horseshoe diamond on his finger. "Who was Sheppard with?" he mused to himself.

"*That's* where we start. But keep in mind, the doctor led two totally different lives: the secret one in New Orleans, Mr. Civic Virtue in St. Petersburg. Our answer could be either here or in Florida."

"What do you want me to do?" Price asked.

"Right now you can help most by *not* calling that press conference."

The p.i. reacted as if I had slapped his face. "I can't sit on my hands," he flared. "I'm being paid to do a job."

"I need this favor," I said.

He stared at me for several seconds. "All right," he said. "I'll hold off for a little while." He didn't like it, though. "I'd think you'd want this press conference," he added.

I didn't intend to argue with him. It was enough that he had agreed to wait.

* * *

"Let's stop by the Marriott," I said to Price when we were seated in the Lincoln.

"A nightcap?"

"I want to show you something."

The Marriott, occupying an entire city block, is one of the finest hotels in New Orleans. But in this city of contrasts the little street that skirted the hotel's south side was Exchange Place, and in the middle of it sat the anything-but-glamorous Cigar's.

Price stopped in front of the pool hall/bar. We stepped out of the car and the scent of stale beer and sidewalk urine attacked our nostrils. A drunk (he could have been twenty years old, or sixty) with a matted beard and greasy hair leaned against the doorless entrance, scratching his crotch. A stream of nasal, twangy, country-western music—somebody on a jukebox whining about unfaithful wives and lost, lonely lives—poured out of this establishment wedged in the heart of the City of Jazz. Inside we could see a torn, filthy linoleum floor (easy to stumble over, an insurance company's nightmare), four stained, time-worn pool tables illuminated by shaded single light bulbs dangling from the ceiling, and a bar lined with neighborhood regulars: a drooling junkie nodding off into his ashtray, a pair of punks sporting muscle shirts and purple tattoos, lots of street hustlers balanced on the fringe of the law and, yes, a lone tourist shooting pool, getting a rush from living on the edge.

"You want that nightcap here?" Price joked.

"Last Thursday we could have had one in this place with Doctor Sheppard."

"You're shitting me."

"I shit you not. This was one of his two favorite spots in New Orleans."

We watched two lost kids tumble out onto Exchange Place, scratching, punching, cursing each other. A third adolescent, joined by the drunk with the matted beard, neither associated with the combatants, desultorily kicked the one who was down.

On the way to dropping me off at Headquarters, Price kept mumbling "Jesus Christ," and shaking his head and punching the steering wheel with a partially balled fist. "Man alive," he said. "This would flabbergast the St. Pete country-club set."

Not Heath and Melerine. I found them in the coffee room pouring cups of what almost every police officer is addicted to. "Court still in session?" Big Hector needled. "You ever make it home?"

"No. I've been with Price."

"The St. Pete gumshoe. How is he?"

"He's planning to offer a ten-thousand-dollar reward."

"Ten thousand? Can I collect?"

"Why? You don't have time to spend all the money the taxpayers throw at you as it is."

Hector raised one eyebrow. "The reward good dead or alive?"

"What do you think?"

"I don't think they'll pay for a stiff."

"I went to Cigar's earlier," I said. "I'd forgotten what a hole it is."

"I've seen you in worse, Dillmann."

"No, you haven't."

"Sure I have."

We stared each other down a moment. "Did you meet the owner?" Hector continued with a grin. "Name's—get this—Billy *Barr.*"

"Bullshit."

"No kidding. Gary and I talked to him this afternoon."

"Did he remember Sheppard?"

"Knows him well. A regular customer who spread the money around pretty good. Said he remembered his being in late last Thursday afternoon, playing pool with a hustler, kid name of Ponce Woods. We heard that name before, from one of those St. Petersburg friends. And listen to this: Sheppard gave this kid an expensive, hand-made pool stick in an alligator carrying case."

"What time did Sheppard leave?" I asked.

"Barr says about 6:00 P.M."

"With Woods?"

"No. He left alone. Woods stayed at the table, breaking in his new stick."

"He might have gone straight to John T's," I said. "He could have met Woods later that night."

"Another name came up. Candy. Barr said Sheppard used to spend a lot of time shooting pool with Candy. He's another one the St. Pete people mentioned."

"Was Candy there last Thursday?"

"Yes. Barr barred him from the joint later that night. Said he caused a disturbance."

Barr barred him? I loved it. More to the point though, two names the St. Petersburg friends provided—Ponce Woods and Candy—had already surfaced. Could Larry Cephas be far away? And were one, two, or all three involved in Sheppard's disappearance? He didn't seem to be afraid of the trio he'd described as friends to his St. Pete neighbors and associates.

"Did you ask Barr about Larry Cephas?"

"Yeah. Says he never heard the name before."

"You trust Barr?"

Big Hector smiled. "Yeah. He's telling the truth. He don't want no heat from us."

"We gave him our cards," Melerine said. "He'll call if he sees Candy or Ponce Woods."

* * *

The graveyard shift started, and I forced myself to shift gears and refocus on my own investigations. I told myself Heath and Melerine didn't need me, to let it go. I'd been up 'round the clock, but I still perked up to greet my best friend Fred Dantagnan when he came in, giving his version of the recent Super Bowl, played in our own Louisiana Superdome, a 27–10 Dallas win over Denver. Randy White and Too Tall Jones were Fred's type of football players: tough.

"Not a very good game," Dantagnan judged. "The Broncos rely too much on finesse."

I shrugged off this observation. Two guys banging heads all day in the trenches constituted Fred's idea of a good game. The way my last twenty-four hours had been going, I felt pretty sure I'd win his approval.

# •3•

"Yes," said John Thoman, owner of John T's, "I remember specifically. Doctor Sheppard was here Thursday night. He had Chicken Pontabla. Mr. Cephas dined with him."

"Would that be Larry Cephas?"

"Yes. A black gentleman. He's a friend of Doctor Sheppard. They've dined here together before."

"How many times before?"

"One other. Just after the start of the new year. That was the first time Mr. Cephas was here."

It was Wednesday, January 25, about 9:00 P.M. I had come in from Slidell a few hours before my shift started to visit John T's where Dr. Mark Sheppard's credit-card receipt indicated he'd eaten after leaving Cigar's. The case had aspects that puzzled and fascinated me. Many of the cases that ran through the department were the usual smoking-gun murder (guy in a bar gets in argument, shoots stranger, puts down weapon, and waits for police to arrive). I wondered what *had* happened to the respected medical doctor with the secret life.

"Did you talk to Doctor Sheppard last Thursday?" I asked Thoman.

"Briefly. We were extremely busy, but I always say hello to the doc."

"How well do you know Larry Cephas?" The names of all three men given to us as friends of Sheppard had now surfaced.

"Not well at all. I've only met him that one other time."

"Can you describe Cephas for me?"

Thoman had been growing exceedingly alarmed. "What's this all about, officer?"

"Sheppard's missing. Your restaurant is one of the last places where he was seen."

"He lives in St. Petersburg. That's probably where he is. He travels back and forth frequently."

"Not likely. He didn't return to his hotel during the weekend, and he missed a scheduled operation Monday morning."

"Oh, my God!" Thoman said, a reaction out of proportion to what I had revealed.

"What is it? What are you thinking?"

"I'm afraid something's drastically wrong. I've gotten to know Doctor Sheppard very well, and missing surgery is totally out of character for him. He's a precise, absolutely punctual man. Calls for reservations a week in advance and then phones back a few days later to confirm."

"This Larry Cephas . . ."

"Oh, yes. He's pretty average. In his mid-twenties, about six feet, I'd say, and very clean cut. He's just a typical nice young man. About Doctor Sheppard. Do you . . ."

"Did they leave together, and at what time?"

"Yes, they did. They arrived here about seven, and left about eight-thirty."

"Do you know where Cephas lives or works?"

"No. But I can try to find out. There aren't many people living in the French Quarter that I don't know."

"Be discreet with anyone you talk to, Mr. Thoman. Here's my card. Please contact me if you learn anything."

He glanced at the card and did a double take when he saw the word *Homicide.* "Detective Dillmann," he said, "you don't believe Doctor Sheppard has been murdered, do you?"

"Right now he's classified as a missing person." I got up from the table where we'd been sitting. "Please, use discretion with those phone calls. Don't alarm anyone."

"About Doctor Sheppard—"

"Don't worry about it. The most normal people turn up missing, and there's usually a simple, straightforward explanation."

"Your card says you're a homicide detective . . ."

"I'm just helping a friend," I lied.

I drove from John T's to the office, hoping the second-shift detective who shared a desk with me would be out. What I was trying to do with the Sheppard case was trace his movements from the moment he arrived in New Orleans. So far, I knew he had checked in at the Ursulines Guest House at approximately 3:00 P.M.; went immediately to play pool at Cigar's until 6:00; and ate at John T's from 7:00 to 8:30. There were brief gaps that I needed to fill, but he had spent a large slice of time in his room that night with a black male. Larry Cephas?

The end result of my efforts, I hoped, and those of Melerine, Heath, and others, was to account for Sheppard's whereabouts right up to the moment of truth—be it murder, suicide, kidnapping, or intentional disappearance.

When I reached the office, Melerine and Heath caught me up on their activities. Heath had just gotten off the phone with Homicide Commander Tom Duffy, who was prepping to brief Chief Morris in the morning. Morris not only reacted swiftly to disasters, but he snuffed out disasters-in-the-making, a category for which he thought this case definitely qualified. Morris envisioned a noisy, nosy p.i. stirring up a storm in the press (touching a sensitive public nerve—most people *did* feel the police responded inadequately to missing-person reports), which would in turn alarm an ever-jittery chamber of commerce representing the most powerful circles in New Orleans. The Crescent City thrived on tourists—especially the well-to-do variety—who weren't supposed to run aground when they came to have fun and pour their money into the local economy. A few highly publicized homicides could strangle the golden goose as surely as the perception of a devastating earthquake in the offing.

Big Hector, into his seventh hour of overtime, wasn't thrilled about briefing me on the Sheppard case, but he might have seen the possibility of some benefits down the road. Maybe I would just take over the lead role, he could have thought. Not many rewards loomed visible, but there'd be plenty of headaches if Morris decided to crank up the pressure. Heath knew how it worked: The media scared the chamber of commerce, these worthies disturbed Morris's serenity, and he blew off steam at Duffy who passed it down the line to the detectives. We didn't have anyone to unload on, unless you counted wives, and we all tried very hard never to do that.

Big Hector also knew a labor-intensive investigation of the Sheppard case didn't stop the other work from coming in. There were eighteen of us in the Homicide unit, trying to unravel the mysteries of murder, and our desks were never clear. We were assigned cases from a rotating roster. If my name headed the list, I drew the investigation, and eighteen murders later, I had to look for another killer, whether or not I had a dozen cases still unsolved. It was a good system—would have been *great* if we'd had sufficient personnel—because it eliminated teams of detectives tripping over one another, restrained individuals from withholding information in hopes of garnering personal acclaim, and because one person could be held accountable. The system eliminated buck-passing and the dilution of blame that rule by committee fosters.

So why did I inject myself into a case that wasn't mine? I think because this whodunit promised a challenge, which is why I became a detective in the first place. I wanted to be part of the case's unraveling, not merely an observer. Also, I couldn't escape it; I had great pride in our unit, the crème de la crème of NOPD. Nobody was a better detective than Saladino, a superstar, and Duffy, Dantagnan, Sergeant Steve London and, hell, I don't know—I wanted a crack at it.

"Gary and I beat the bushes all day for Ponce Woods," Heath said.

"Any luck?"

"Luck? What kind of luck? Woods's old lady is trying to serve him with divorce papers and he's on the run. His mother hasn't seen him for two weeks. She says he's been staying on North Claiborne with his older brother Cleveland, but no one was home when we checked."

"Woods have any prior arrests?"

"Typical. Possession of weed. Armed robbery."

Armed robbery fit the profile we often found attached to a killer. Generally, an individual doesn't start his crime career with a murder. He moves up through lesser offenses.

"How about Cigar's?"

"We went back there. I figured Woods might be practicing with that new cue stick. Barr says Woods usually comes in every afternoon, but not today. We'll try to pop him tomorrow."

"I may have a lead on Larry Cephas," I said, and Big

Hector's ears pricked up. "I stopped by John T's earlier tonight and learned that Cephas had dinner there with Sheppard on Thursday. They left about eight-thirty. The owner can ID him."

"So Cephas is the last person with Sheppard," Heath said.

"Probably. But I'm not sure. Jim Owens at the Ursulines can tell us if he was the guy who spent the night."

"This Cephas, is he a character?"

"I don't think so. I'll try to find him tonight. If he's legit, he'll probably be at home."

Criminal Investigation Division Desk Sergeant Fred Turlein called me almost the moment I sat down at my desk. "Dillmann," he said, "this guy Price has been on the horn every fifteen minutes. Isn't that the p.i. from St. Pete?"

"The same."

"Call him at the Marriott. He's driving me crazy."

I phoned Price, aware that if Henry Morris found out I dealt with this p.i., he would nail my hide to the wall. Morris, who had worked his way through the ranks, ruled CID with an iron hand. Ultimately he became chief of police, respected and feared, a cop's cop who believed an old-time beat patrolman with neighborhood ties was a more effective crime fighter than a whole bank of Super Cosmos XV computers that did everything but light a detective's cigarettes. Legwork and more legwork solved most crimes, Morris preached, and he was right.

"What's up, John?" Price asked eagerly, trying to honor my suggestion that he sit tight. It wasn't an easy task for this make-it-happen go-getter. I later learned Price had carried out a few assignments for the CIA, and owned several exotic Maxwell Smart-type gadgets: state-of-the-art bugging and debugging devices, a flashlight that temporarily blinded anyone it got shone on, a tiny gun he concealed behind his belt buckle. Indeed, in New Orleans, Price walked around more heavily armed than I did. Besides the belt-buckle weapon, he sported a .38 Chief Special secured in an ankle holster. He had permits for both guns, of course, but that fact didn't make me more secure.

I smile whenever I think of the aging yuppie Price. He belonged to a variety of organizations it would never have occurred to me to join, including the chamber of commerce, the American Association of Criminologists, the Florida Association of Private Investigators, the American Detective Association, and the International Police Congress.

"We're making some headway," I said. "We've identified a few people, and have some good addresses."

"Have you found the guy who was seen with Doc on Friday morning?"

"We think so, but we haven't interviewed him yet."

"I went to Cigar's today. I—"

"You wear your Rolex?"

"No. Left it in the room. Anyway, I need to know what Sheppard's friends look like. You got any pictures?"

"What did you do in Cigar's?"

"Looked around, drank a few beers, tried to pick up on something."

"Did you?"

"Almost got picked up myself. Somebody wearing a dress who had arms hairier than mine."

"Did you spot a pool player with an alligator carrying case?"

"No. An alligator cue case in Cigar's. That I would have noticed. Like a tuxedo at a mud pull. Look, John, I know you're on the midnight shift. I took a nap this afternoon and I'm ready to move. How about picking me up and we'll find these people tonight?"

"I don't know," I said. "I'll come over after roll call. We'll talk."

I knew Price itched to start proving to Betty Woodard and Joe Bradham that their money was well spent, and the quickest way to do this meant holding a bell-ringing press conference highlighted by the announcement of a $10,000 reward.

Just as smoke implies fire, publicity gives the *impression* of activity. So far we had kept a lid on any sensationalism by evincing little indication of police involvement, and if Dr. Sheppard had been killed by an acquaintance in New Orleans, the murderer likely believed himself safe. However, when the story broke in the *Times-Picayune* and reward posters hung from every lamppost, the perpetrator would become more cautious, and therefore more difficult to apprehend. As matters stood now, experience taught, a killer's confidence might be so high that he'd boast to friends, a not unusual occurrence, though the memory of those "friends" could come back to haunt him during a lifetime at Angola State Prison, or on his way to Louisiana's electric chair, after they "traded" the murder he committed for a lesser sentence for themselves.

The truth is, when the identity of a murderer isn't self-evident, the crime is usually solved through a snitch. I have seen brother turn in brother, a mother give up her son, a wife her husband. Valuable as experience is, a detective would be better off giving it up than surrendering his sources of information.

In any case, NOPD didn't need publicity. Not yet. Not until we interviewed every possible suspect in the case *before* any of them realized the possible extreme danger in cooperating with us.

Preventing publicity was why I agreed to visit Price. A reward poster and media coverage would necessarily contain details that could fatally flaw a subsequent prosecution. For example, a confession that included a description of the clothes Dr. Sheppard wore at the time of his disappearance would be infinitely more persuasive if the information hadn't already been printed in the newspaper or recounted on a radio or TV news broadcast. *Anything,* if confessed to, gets challenged by a defense attorney when it's already public knowledge. Defendants who have never seen more than the sports page of a newspaper are portrayed as bookworms by their lawyers. What a detective needs are facts only the killer could know.

After telling Price I would stop by for him about 1:00 A.M., I wandered over to our lone computer terminal, which was hooked into National Crime Information Center (NCIC) records, plus local and state data banks. A treasure trove, this computer could spit out information on anyone who even had a driver's license. I entered the name C-E-P-H-A-S, L-A-R-R-Y, and waited. By matching John Thoman's physical description of Sheppard's dinner partner to the computer entry, I determined that the Larry Cephas I searched for had no criminal record and a last known address of 2335 Ursulines, on the outskirts of the French Quarter.

Since I had called the computer to attention, I decided to go further. I programmed the alias index and entered C-A-N-D-Y. After a few seconds, a multi-page list rolled out of the printer. It looked like this, the first entry being the arrest record number:

```
XM.3109.00063100 CANDY WF 08/28/53
XM.3109.00204010 CANDY NM 08/12/53
XM.3109.00270110 CANDY NF 02/01/54
XM.3109.00276910 CANDY WF 09/24/51
XM.3109.00081430 CANDY WF 03/03/52
```

```
XM.3109.00389540 CANDY NF 01/05/61
XM.3109.00313640 CANDY WM 01/15/54
XM.3109.00045090 CANDY NM 05/03/56
XM.3109.00045890 CANDY NF 12/06/48
XM.3109.00166660 CANDY WM 11/05/34
```

On and on it went, through seventy-nine more entries for Candy. Some of them could be eliminated immediately. The first name on the list belonged to a white female (WF), the third to a black female (NF), the seventh to a white male (WM). Number 10 was not only white but born in 1934, much too old.

Candy turned out to be a nickname more preferred by women than men. There were fifteen black men on file who used the alias and could, from the scant information we possessed, be the individual we sought.

I folded the printout and put it in my desk for future reference. So far, all I had to indicate Candy might be a key to Sheppard's disappearance was the doctor's mentioning him to Edward White as a friend. When and if something else developed on Candy, I'd return to the computer and recall each of the fifteen black males. I would enter the arrest record number and obtain a real name, address, Social Security number, physical description, prior arrests and convictions, plus the places he'd been picked up. But tonight it made sense to postpone attacking what promised to be a mountain of paper.

After the roll call, Saladino and Dantagnan cut me off at the pass. "Let's have some coffee," Pascal suggested.

"I can't," I said. "I've got an appointment."

"What's so important that it can't wait until after coffee?" Dantagnan asked. Fred—pal, partner, the godfather of my children—had felt an obligation to protect me since the 1960s when we rode a patrol car together. I didn't mind.

I wanted it. We had helped pull each other through many tight spots, and there was no one I trusted at my back more than the no-nonsense, powerful Dantagnan.

And Saladino, the murder cop we tried to emulate, the one who got me into Homicide in the first place, he blocked my path also. Why were these two so eager to talk?

It once took Saladino *twelve years* to solve a murder case, but solve it he did, long after most detectives would have given up. Two armed robbers shot up a New Orleans tavern, wounding eight people, three of them fatally. Two of the dead victims were the parents of a New Orleans cop.

With virtually no clues to pursue, Saladino nonetheless kept digging. He never let himself forget the bloodbath in that bar. Ten years later, armed only with a prison inmate's recollection of overhearing a conversation about *different* homicides, he matched the bullets taken from the bodies in the bar to bullets found at other unsolved murders.

Two years after this, with FBI assistance, Saladino's evidence led to convictions for *eight* murders, including the three in the tavern. Other victims included a bank teller, a nun, and a priest. Saladino's remarkable skills solved a multiple murder case even the most optimistic superior believed hopeless.

"I have to talk to Dick Price," I said, trying to sidestep these two.

A solemn expression spread across Saladino's dark face. "Dick Price, huh?" His eyes narrowed. He blew a poisonous blast of cigar smoke. "Tell me, Dillmann, do Sheppard's family and friends realize there is almost no chance that he's alive?"

"I don't know, Sal."

"Chief Morris has organized the world," Pascal said. "He's activated three shifts to look for seven-cent scumbags in the Quarter, and now you're rendezvousing with

Mannix. We'll all work on this missing-person case for six months, and Sheppard's body will turn up in the Honey Island swamp." He smiled bitterly, blew another noxious cloud of smoke. "Possession is nine-tenths of the law. Think, Dillmann: When the body is brought out of that swamp, St. Tammany Parish Sheriff's Office will investigate, Dick Price will take his show over there, and we'll turn our case files over to them."

"What are you saying?"

"I'm betting, my friend, that you're wasting a lot of time."

"You think we shouldn't be working this case?"

"No, goddammit! I'm saying be prepared for the outcome. Don't ever believe you'll solve a homicide without a body. And if that body's not yours, you're history, and so is all the work you've put in. I'm not saying don't look at it. I'm saying, don't miss coffee."

The voice of experience from Mr. Cynical. I learned so much from Pascal, but the negativism—realism, if you will—I tried not to let capture me. I had to keep telling myself I did good, that catching murderers made a difference, that even the *chance* of catching one made the effort worthwhile. If we waited the six months, say, that it took to find Sheppard's body, it would be too late for everyone, including St. Tammany. Everything would be too old and cold—the evidence and the memories of witnesses.

"All right, all right," I said. "HoJo's for coffee. When you guys set your minds, you stick like white on rice."

"More like buzzards on a gut wagon," Dantagnan said, briskly rubbing his palms together and rasping out a ghoulish snicker. Fred had an endless repertoire of graveyard humor, collected during many years of viewing the dead. That was his escape valve, his method of preventing hundreds of stone-cold faces from reaching through the dark recesses of his memory, pleading for justice and revenge.

We went to Howard Johnson's on Old Gentilly Highway. I had solved a double murder there, two state-protected witnesses blown away execution-style on the orders of a drug czar against whom they were scheduled to testify. Going for coffee at HoJo's had no connection. It was open twenty-four hours a day, handy, and at this hour inhabited mostly by cops who put their guns on the table and talked shop. Pascal wanted to go fishing this weekend. I said maybe, and we joked about our last time out.

Ten homicide detectives had juggled schedules and chipped in fifty dollars apiece to charter a boat. Our destination: Venice, Louisiana, where the mouth of the Mississippi River empties into the Gulf of Mexico. This convergence of fresh and salt waters is home to a bountiful supply of speckled trout, redfish, pompano, and red snapper.

Buddy Pons, our favorite skipper, a weathered salt perfect for the title role in *The Old Man and the Sea,* moored the boat to an oil platform and announced we had lucked out on a day made for fishing.

A rough-looking, unshaven lot after crawling out of bed and into favorite "lucky" fishing grubbies long before dawn, many of us stood on deck with a wake-up beer in hand, definitely not receptive to the big hammerhead shark that surfaced fifteen yards out and began circling the boat. This marine marauder, notorious for frightening away any fish in the vicinity, lived up to its reputation. We didn't get a nibble.

Changing from cut squid to shrimp didn't help, and nobody was in the mood for Dantagnan's pat line: "If we don't catch anything, we can always eat the bait." The sun burned hotter and so did the members of the murder squad, cursing under their breath and casting angry glances at Buddy Pons up on the bridge.

"Damn!" our skipper said. "I can't believe I didn't bring my rifle today."

We all looked at one another.

"Anyone happen to be carrying his pistol?" Buddy asked innocently. It was the wrong question to ask this crew.

Ten guns gleamed in the sunlight and fired a thunderous volley loud enough to awaken Davy Jones himself. All of us missed (had Duffy witnessed this display of poor marksmanship, he would have had us on the target range the next day), but we scared the shark away and got on with some serious fishing.

Saladino presided in Howard Johnson's like a mob boss, greeting various cops, plainclothes and uniformed, who came to our table to pay him tribute. Sal, always smiling, talking in his high-pitched voice, had words of advice for everybody. When the salutations were finished and we sat alone, he returned to the Sheppard case. "Is this doctor as rich as I hear?" he asked.

"Maybe richer. He owns four vintage Rolls-Royces."

"No shit?" He emitted another smoke cloud that set me coughing, my eyes on fire. "Goes to show you, Dillmann, a bullet don't care how much you're worth."

Price paced for warmth, the collar of his coat pulled over his ears against a brisk winter wind, when I pulled to a stop at 1:30 A.M. in front of the Marriott.

"You're late, John," he said, looking at his Rolex.

"A guy I admire said to take time and smell the flowers."

"What flowers? You got a lead?"

"Get in. We'll drive."

I wheeled the plainclothes 1975 Ford LTD out onto Airline Highway west toward Moissant International Airport. I could just have easily have taken him north to Lake Pontchartrain and across the Causeway, at twenty-six miles the longest bridge in the world, but the scenery on Airline seemed more appropriate to the case we wrestled with. Here were long lines of shabby motels, a couple of miles of red-light joints, made famous later by television evangelist Jimmy Swaggart. Once the major route linking New Orleans and Baton Rouge, Airline Highway fell on hard times with the completion of Interstate 10.

"John," Price said, "what are we doing out here? I thought we were going to the Quarter to find Woods, Cephas, and Candy."

"We can't, Dick. I know you mean well, but look what you've accomplished already. Your arrival here prompted Chief Morris to get the entire Homicide unit involved in this investigation. You have to remember Doctor Sheppard is officially a missing person. This type of investigation has to be taken in steps, and though I want to work with you, you need to play by our rules: Share information with us and assist, but don't hinder us with counterproductive actions hastily implemented."

"What are you talking about?"

"The press conference and reward."

"They're great ideas. Especially the reward. Ten thousand is nothing to sniff at. My phone will be ringing off the hook with information."

"Probably. But how good will that information be? If Sheppard's dead, and the killer has kept his mouth shut, your reward won't get *him* to call."

"Of course not. But if he's run his head, it could break the case."

"And if he hasn't, it could mess everything up permanently. You willing to take that chance?"

"How long do you want me to hold off?"

"A couple of days. Give us time to locate and interview these people. Remember, they may not be involved. Sheppard considered them friends. But if one or more is responsible, your publicity would tip our hand."

"Okay. But I feel foolish sitting around."

I cautioned myself to be sensitive. Price had a job to do, a living to make, and I needed to show concern for his plight. "I understand how you feel, Dick," I said. "Just do it our way for a little while."

"Can you give me something to pass on to Joe Bradham?"

"I think so. But first see if you can hurry up on that copy of Sheppard's will. Also, do you have any contacts with the phone company?"

"What do you need?"

"A record of Sheppard's long-distance calls. Dating back to July of 1977 should do nicely. It'll give us six months."

"No problem." I'd hear these words from Price often. "I'll do what I can on the will. I don't think it'll help."

"Maybe. Maybe not. But if the three so-called friends are innocent, and Sheppard is dead, our killer could be in St. Petersburg."

"You're thinking of Cabrera, the doctor who was here at the same time as Sheppard."

"I'd want to look at anybody with a money motive."

Price shook his head. Clearly he thought I was on the wrong track. "What can you give me?" he said.

"We should have Cephas and Woods by tonight. Then we'll know where we're headed. I'll call you as soon as we find them."

"I guess that'll have to do."

"What about Sheppard?" I asked. "Anything more on his background?"

"It's kind of sad. His mother and father are dead, and he doesn't have sisters or brothers. No close relatives at all."

"He had good friends. Those people who came from St. Pete are concerned about his welfare."

"Yeah. And lots of associates at St. Anthony's who swear by him. I guess you never know."

I thought about that will. "I really think," I said, "you'll be driving me around St. Pete."

"It would be a pleasure. You can stay at my place. Meet my girlfriend—Twinkle."

"Twinkle?"

"Yeah. Terrific gal. Full of life. You'll love her."

Twinkle?

# • 4 •

PASCAL Saladino intended his advice about not missing irretrievable moments with friends also to apply to the one unit more important and precious still, my family. At best, over the past several days, I had lurched into our Slidell home about 9:00 A.M. after the hour drive from New Orleans, given Diane a tired hug, and fallen in bed. When I woke up in the late afternoon, I had a bite to eat and headed back to work.

In 1967 I had been part of the last police training class to qualify for the sixteen-year pension fund, offered because the city experienced difficulty recruiting people qualified to be officers. The reason for the problem: The pay in 1967 was $300 a month, and the new cop had to buy his own gun, equipment, and uniform. I had joined the force at age twenty with the understanding that I would quit at thirty-six (I waited till thirty-eight), take the pension, and find another job. The plan I worked out with Diane looked good in the abstract, but there was never enough money, so often I moonlighted—at this time I directed security for the Bourbon Orleans Hotel. This job, and others, plus piles of unpaid extra hours on homicide cases, resulted in very little time for Diane, my son Todd, ten, and five-year-old daughter Amy. If I did the job right, I couldn't avoid the many, many hours of overtime. I could have labored twenty-four hours a day and never caught up.

I woke at 3:00 P.M. this Thursday, January 26, 1978, the one-week anniversary of Dr. Sheppard's arrival in New Orleans, and had coffee with Diane in the den. As always, she asked what current case primarily occupied my attention.

I told her about Dr. Sheppard. She already knew about my other open investigations. Quick to pick up on the slightest change in a suspect's expression, still I failed to notice my wife's face growing exceedingly grim. Ever since becoming the youngest homicide detective in New Orleans history, I had used Diane as a sounding board, talking through my cases and in the telling clarifying points in my own mind. She always had great compassion for the victim, which made my own job easier—obtaining justice for the dead (yes, mainly for the dead, because the majority of murderers wouldn't kill again), and *maybe* as a deterrent, though not often, since criminals don't usually consider the consequences.

When a homicide isn't committed in the heat of passion, but carefully planned, the perpetrator *thinks he'll get away with it:* The cops aren't very smart (perhaps true, but they're usually brighter than the killer), or his plan is foolproof ("Damn," a murderer will say later, "I was really unlucky. Who could have figured a guy standing outside would write down my license number?"). Just as rare as the bad guy considering the likelihood of being caught is the murderer who experiences remorse. The killer is seldom sorry, though he may put on a very convincing show for a judge. He regrets only that he was captured.

Justice for the victim was my prime motivator. I always put myself in his shoes, and knew I would hope someone cared enough to avenge the taking of my own life, if it ever came to that.

"What about Doctor Sheppard's family?" Diane asked, nothing ingenuous in the question. She was concerned.

"His mother and father are dead," I said. "He has no siblings. We don't think there are even any aunts or uncles. Nobody."

"That's terrible. Do you really think he's dead?"

"Honestly, Diane, I believe he is."

"Well, maybe you're wrong."

"Maybe."

She sipped her coffee, staring into the cup.

"John?"

"Yes."

"Are you working at the Bourbon Orleans tonight?"

"Yes. But there's a witness I need to find first. Fred will cover for me."

"So you'll be leaving soon?"

"Quick as I can get dressed."

"Can't you wait until Todd gets home from school? He needs to see you at home, at least for a few minutes."

*Now* I noticed the darkened face. Too late, I braced myself for the gathered storm.

"Sure," I said, trying to rally. "I'll be dressed before Todd gets in, and I'll spend some time with him before I leave."

"Something puzzles me, John."

"What's that?"

"Why are you working on this case? Doctor Sheppard's missing. You said yourself that he might be alive."

"No, Diane. I said he's probably dead."

"Okay. But why you? Why is it *always* you?"

"It's not always me. Everybody's working on it. You know the static we'll get from this. The guy's a tourist. A wealthy one. Morris wants it solved."

"Chief Morris may want it solved, but you can't work on this or any other case if you're sick."

"Sick? I feel great."

"You're working two jobs."

"I have to. You know that. We've rehashed this a hundred times. Five more years and I make my pension. We've lasted this long. When I retire from the force I'll find a normal job with normal hours and the pension will be a nice supplement. Don't worry, we'll be fine."

"John, you don't look good, and frankly, a lot of the problem is you. You can't handle every case in New Orleans. You're not Superman, you know."

Superman? It wasn't the first time she had upbraided me with the same reference. I wasn't macho, didn't believe I could fight ten people at once, didn't even have a particularly high self-image. At this stage of my life I did consider myself a competent murder investigator—I had a knack for it—but Superman?

"Listen . . ." I began.

"You listen, John. You're killing yourself. You can't work in moderation. One day you're just going to keel over."

"That's . . ." I started my defense, but blessedly we heard Todd open the front door and yell, "I'll be out in a minute," to a playmate. The sound of his feet coming through the house tabled the debate and smoothed our furrowed brows. Diane and I adhered to several rules laid down early in our marriage, and one of them involved holding no acrimonious discussions in front of the children. Todd, our energetic fourth-grader, caught me up on school and his friends while I downed a ham sandwich and glass of milk.

On the drive over Lake Pontchartrain I thought about Dantagnan and myself. Maybe Fred had a better handle on his home front than I did on mine. He worked overtime when a case absolutely demanded it—a witness or suspect about to skip town, the danger of a killer striking again—

but he made sure to allot plenty of time to his family. A pat on the back from Henry Morris or adding another letter of commendation to the dozens he'd already earned counted for nothing in light of his marriage. I didn't believe I loved Diane less than Fred loved Bea, though an observer, not knowing either of us, might have judged differently.

I swung by Larry Cephas's white, single-story, well-kept frame house on Ursulines, a proud residential area of old homes, and families who had lived there for generations.

A man about twenty-five years old answered my knock on the door, a tall, slender, light-complexioned black with a baby face and short-cropped hair, dressed in jeans and a cardigan.

"Larry Cephas?" I said.

"I'm Larry. Can I help you?"

"My name is John Dillmann. I'm a detective with the New Orleans Police Department and I'd like to ask you a few questions."

Cephas laughed. "Police Department? You sure you got the right place?"

"Yes, I'm sure. I won't take much of your time, but it's extremely important."

"Come inside. I can't imagine how I can help you."

I stepped into a warm, comfortable living room and sat in a red velour easy chair. The TV was tuned to an "I Love Lucy" rerun. Something told me I wouldn't be interviewing a murderer, unless he was shrewder and more cunning than any I'd yet encountered.

"Do you know Doctor Mark Sheppard?" I asked.

"Yes, I do." Not a quiver of alarm. "As a matter of fact, we had dinner at John T's a week ago. He's a medical doctor in St. Petersburg, Florida."

"How long have you known Doctor Sheppard?"

"About three weeks. We have something in common. We both love to shoot pool."

"The last time you saw him was the dinner at John T's last week?"

"Well . . ."

His hesitation set alarms ringing in my head. I thought I knew what it meant. *Always,* I had learned, *err on the side of caution.*

"Larry," I said, "I want you to take a ride over to police headquarters with me. We'll be more comfortable there."

"I'm comfortable here."

But he soon wouldn't be, I suspected. "Larry, do you live alone?"

"No. I live with my parents."

"Take a ride with me to my office. We need to discuss sensitive matters you might not want your mother and father to hear. I think you know what I mean."

"Will it take long?"

"I don't think so."

"Will you bring me back?"

I found it remarkable how often people asked this question. They faced an unpleasant ordeal, but what they feared most was having to walk home.

"Of course I will."

We drove in the unmarked car to Broad Street, and I took him up to the murder room on the third floor. No signs advertised HOMICIDE, so likely he didn't know where we were, though he might have guessed if he'd read the occasional gallows-humor signs hung on the walls. For instance: "Our Day Begins When Yours Ends."

We sat opposite each other at my battered desk—he in a chair that literally dozens of killers had occupied. I felt virtually certain Larry Cephas wouldn't be added to the list.

"*This* is your office?" he asked.

"Yeah," I said, and smiled. He had a sense of humor, too, a trait not prominent in murderers.

"Larry," I said, "Doctor Sheppard is missing, and we're afraid that he's dead."

"What? How . . ."

"Wait a minute." I knew what I had to do next would scare him, but there wasn't any way around it. "Please don't say anything until I ask. Don't interrupt. You may have been the last person to see Doctor Sheppard alive. I'm going to have to read you your rights."

"My rights?" No humor now. He stared at me with wide-open, disbelieving eyes.

"It's just a formality, but you need to listen very carefully. Make sure you understand what I'm about to tell you." I let this sink in, then continued. "You need not make any statements, that is, you have the right to remain silent. Anything you say can and will be used against you in a court of law. You have the right to have an attorney present at the time of any questioning or the giving of any statement. If you cannot afford an attorney, the court will appoint one to represent you." I waited a moment, then asked: "Do you understand these rights?"

"I understand, but I don't know why I'm a suspect in anything. Because I know Mark Sheppard, is that it?"

*No,* I thought. *It's because you're the last person who saw the missing man alive. It's because if I'm wrong and you* are *guilty, a defense lawyer will make certain no jury ever hears what you tell me.* Out loud I said, "Will you waive your right to have an attorney present so we can continue this interview?"

"I'm willing to tell you anything. I want this cleared up right now."

"You're gay, aren't you, Larry?"

"Yes, I am."

"You say you first met Doctor Sheppard three weeks ago?"

"Yes."

"I'd like you to tell me the circumstances of that meeting."

"He saw me at the Green Lantern Bar and bought me a drink."

I knew the place: the corner of Barracks and Royal, a respectable enough spot.

"What did you do at the Green Lantern?"

"Had a few drinks. Talked. Doctor Sheppard invited me to shoot a game of pool with him. What can I say? I was flattered by his attention. We became friends. He's a very nice man."

"Did you stay with him that night?"

"No."

"When was the next time you saw Doctor Sheppard?"

"Last Thursday at John T's. We'd exchanged phone numbers. He called me from St. Petersburg and invited me to dinner."

"Where did he call you?"

"At home."

My belief in Cephas's non-involvement in Sheppard's disappearance grew by the minute. He replied to questions as though he had nothing to hide, the way an individual would if he thought "coming clean" would put an uncomfortable situation behind him.

"Did you meet at John T's?"

"Yes. He arrived before I did."

"Did Doctor Sheppard happen to mention what he'd been doing since he'd arrived in New Orleans?"

"He said he'd come straight from shooting some pool."

"Did he say who he played with?"

"No. But he has several friends in the city. He didn't mention names."

"What did you do after dinner? Where did you go?"

"We walked over to a bar. Lafitte's in Exile, on Bourbon Street."

"Anything unusual happen at Lafitte's?"

"Nothing. We had a couple of drinks and shot a few games of pool."

"Then what?"

"That night?"

"Yeah. That night."

He decided to come right out with it. "We left the bar and spent the night together."

"Where?"

"A guest house. It's on Ursulines. I can't recall the name."

"Do you remember anything about the place?"

"There was this big iron door and you could only get in or out with a key. Oh, right. Doctor Sheppard had this big statue in his room. Andrew Jackson, I think."

"What time did you leave the guest house?" Questions to which I already knew the answer served as a good measure of the truthfulness of other replies.

"About seven-thirty in the morning. I had to get up early to take a civil service exam."

"Did Doctor Sheppard unlock the iron door to let you out?"

"We left together. He was going to the French Market for coffee and donuts."

"Do you know if he intended to meet someone?"

"He didn't say anything about that. He was alone when I saw him last."

"Where was that?"

"The corner of Royal and Ursulines. He said he'd look me up the next time he came to the city."

This had been Friday morning, and Sheppard's return flight to St. Petersburg wasn't until Sunday. Clearly he had other plans that he didn't discuss with Larry Cephas.

"So the last you saw him was at seven-forty-five that morning?"

"About then. Right."

"Did Doctor Sheppard seem nervous to you? Was he upset about anything?"

"No. Not at all. He was in a very upbeat mood."

"Larry, what can you tell me about Mark Sheppard? Anything at all might help."

"Only that he's a doctor, an anesthesiologist, and seemed to be a very sincere person. He appeared very interested in the civil service exam I was going to take, and he told me he was sure I'd do well."

"One more thing. Did Doctor Sheppard mention anything about a will?"

"A will? No."

"Larry," I said, "do you have any objections to taking a polygraph examination?"

"You mean a lie detector test?"

"Yes."

"You don't believe what I told you?"

"I do believe you, but that doesn't count. Mark my words, Larry, Doctor Sheppard will probably turn up dead, and since you are the last person known to have seen him alive, you can head off a lot of future hassle by cooperating now. Think about what lies down the road if his body is found. He's gay. He's got important friends who will be demanding answers. There's going to be a lot of heat. Do yourself a favor and take the test."

"I'm telling you the truth, but I'm afraid of those machines. I don't trust them. Besides, I'm nervous. What if that gadget shows I'm lying. I'd be in a mess of trouble."

"The polygraph knows the difference. It doesn't matter if you're nervous."

In truth, test results are only as good as the polygraph operator. The main ways to "beat the box" are to have an incompetent tester, be a pathological liar, or be mellowed out on sedative medication. We had one of the best polygraph operators in the South in Lieutenant Gene Fields, and Larry Cephas was neither a pathological liar nor on drugs, from what I could judge.

"Okay," Cephas said. "I'll take a chance. Let's get on with it."

I called Fields at his home and he said he'd meet us shortly in the polygraph office on the third floor to administer the exam.

A session with the polygraph consists of four tests. After a practice run, the same set of questions is asked three more times. Fields asked Cephas 1) Are you black? and 2) Are you a male? Cephas would never lie providing these self-evident answers, and the results of his truthful replies were then compared to the responses given to four questions I wanted answered. One was, "Did you kill Doctor Mark Sheppard?" a second was, "Do you know anyone who might have been involved in Doctor Sheppard's disappearance?" and the third and fourth were variations of the first two, designed to determine if he had any knowledge whatever of the doctor's fate.

To none of the queries did Cephas give any indication of deception. I drove him home, thanked him, shook his hand, and went to the Bourbon Orleans to relieve Fred.

The positive part of the episode was learning virtually all of Dr. Sheppard's movements from the time of his arrival in New Orleans on the 19th until 7:45 A.M. on the 20th when he bade farewell to Cephas. No one at the French Market remembered him, a not unusual development since this New Orleans landmark is one of the most popular spots in the city. I guessed, however, that he never reached that destination. He stopped somewhere, or was waylaid.

I called Big Hector at his home, and he asked me to "cut a daily" for him, i.e., write a report on the Cephas interview for the Sheppard case file. I asked if he'd found Ponce Woods.

"Early this afternoon," Heath said. "Gary and I ran him down at Cigar's. He was practicing with his new pool cue."

"What's his connection with Sheppard?"

"They met last summer in Cigar's. Sheppard challenged him to a pool game, which I suspect was a mistake. Today Gary and I got a sample of Woods's hustle. Looks like he's a pretty good shooter. I have a feeling Sheppard was out of his league."

"That's obvious, Hector."

"I'm talking about pool. These guys are sharks. They hustle for a living. Sheppard was probably an easy mark."

"So they met at Cigar's last summer?"

"Yeah. Woods had just been popped for that armed robbery, lost his job pumping gas at a Tenneco station, and was out on bond hustling pool when Sheppard approached him and asked to play. The doc lost a few games, bing, bing, bing, and said he'd like to take lessons from Woods."

"Lessons?"

"Right. Pool lessons. Twenty dollars an hour." Hector snorted. "Evidently Woods and Sheppard became pretty good friends. Whenever Sheppard was in town—and, get this, he'd been coming every two or three weeks since at least last summer—he went to Cigar's and hung out there."

"What's your opinion of Woods?"

"I think he's leveling with us. It seems he genuinely liked Sheppard. Tried to see that nobody ripped him off. Acted as a sort of protector."

"What about last Thursday? Did the doctor seem worried about anything?"

"Not according to Woods. They shot pool, just like every other time. He showed us the cue and alligator carrying case Sheppard gave him."

"What was the purpose of the gift?"

"I gather it's the sort of thing Sheppard did. Woods said he never carried a lot of money with him, very careful about that, but he'd give presents to people he liked."

"He see Sheppard after Thursday afternoon?"

"No. He thinks he's home in Florida."

I rubbed my eyes and sighed. "Not much help, was he?"

"He said one interesting thing: Regulars at Cigar's often tried to tap Sheppard for loans. The doc listened to a lot of sob stories, acted sympathetic, but he seldom shelled out. Maybe somebody got hot over a turndown."

"Could be, Hector. But it had to happen the next day. Sheppard spent the entire night with Larry Cephas."

"Yeah." Heath didn't sound happy. "We'll run Woods in the box tomorrow, but I don't expect anything."

"Dead-end city," I said. My chest hurt and my head ached. I figured I'd be okay if I just had a solid lead to pursue, but the case, like Sheppard, had just gone *poof.*

Where to next? We had about run out of any avenue detectives normally pursue, and though we suspected murder we didn't have a body. Morris would soon be demanding results, but they couldn't be materialized from thin air.

Well, they might not have to be. The common-sense approach to solving a murder—any crime, really—involved checking first into the ordinary and obvious. When that failed, and usually it didn't, a good investigator cranked the operation into a higher gear and did the *extra*ordinary.

# •5•

On January 27, 1978, with every homicide detective who could find a free moment assisting, the search for Dr. Mark Sheppard accelerated. Uniformed officers distributed photographs reproduced from the driver's license of the missing man to all the districts in the city, which meant ultimately that every cop in New Orleans would see it. In addition, outside reinforcements were asked to aid in the hunt:

- Captain Charrier of the St. Bernard Parish Sheriff's Office agreed to assist by searching remote areas in his jurisdiction southeast of New Orleans, which included Chalmette, numerous fishing, shrimping, and oystering villages, and vast stretches of marsh land.
- Dr. Sheppard's credit-card companies pledged to notify us of any purchases charged on 1/20/78 or later.
- Price discovered that Dr. Sheppard had brought to New Orleans an extremely valuable gold Patek Philippe wristwatch, and we provided a detailed de-

scription to every pawnbroker and jeweler in the city.

- The Sanitation Department's Raymond Bodenheimer promised to have his men check every landfill and incinerator in New Orleans.
- Assistant Chief Ray Moorhouse of U.S. Coast Guard Intelligence ordered his service personnel to search wharf areas and the shoreline of Lake Pontchartrain.
- Photographs of Dr. Sheppard were delivered to hotels, taxi companies, the Baptist Mission, Salvation Army, YMCA, airport employees, and rental car agencies.
- Richard Boneno of the Public Belt Road/railroad promised to check boxcars and trash bins along the Mississippi River.
- Joe Lala of L&N Railroad said his employees would check the company's boxcars and tracks.
- Ditto Jim Skinner of the M&P Railroad.
- And finally, the Harbor Police launched a search of wharves and wharf aprons.

Swamps. Marshes. The Mississippi River. Lake Pontchartrain. These have been favorite dumping grounds for bodies since New Orleans was founded. Sergeant Paul Drouant, who supervised much of the search, muttered to Tom Duffy, "If this guy Sheppard turns out to be on vacation, he'll never have to worry about being killed. I'll do it myself."

Hospitals had already been contacted, of course, and an alert sent out locally and nationwide over the NCIC computer. We didn't want Judge Crater-type jokes in New Orleans.

The case nagged at me throughout the graveyard shift. Despite Herculean efforts (the enlistment of an army to locate an AWOL?), we had accomplished nothing in New Orleans. I worried we were barking up the wrong tree—our answers were to be found somewhere else.

Lieutenant Duffy came in at 8:00 A.M., and I stationed myself to be first into his office. "Tom, could I see you for a minute?"

"Sure, John. I hope you got some good news. I can't take any more bad."

"The Sheppard case. I think we're looking in the wrong place."

"What do you mean?"

"We've been concentrating on Sheppard's activities in New Orleans. None of them have led us to the answer. We know he led two completely different lives, depending on the city he was in. So maybe the problem isn't here."

"You know something I don't?"

"It may be nothing. But it seems odd that he makes out a will, flies to New Orleans, and suddenly disappears. Maybe it's coincidence."

"When did he do the will?"

"Two days before he came here."

"Where did you learn this?"

"Dick Price."

"Arrgh." Duffy groaned.

"I'm saying we might need to do a good background check in St. Pete. Maybe there's *another* side to Doctor Sheppard."

Duffy leaned back in his chair and cocked his feet up on his desk. "If the weather stays like this, I might go fishing tomorrow."

That was just Duffy. He hadn't forgotten me or our discussion, and momentarily sidetracking the matter gave him space to think. Duffy loved fishing, had his own boat, often went out by himself and caught more than a hundred trout or redfish, perfectly legal in 1978 and a delicious treat to share with friends and relatives. Yes, one hundred, and that was on the days when he didn't knock himself out for a big haul. Fishermen in south Louisiana don't usually boast about this to people from other parts of the country who think it's just another exaggerated fish tale. That's fine: It leaves more for the locals to catch and enjoy.

"By God, I *ought* to go fishing," Duffy said, his Irish face wistful, open, filled with the anticipation of a little boy. But of course he wasn't Huckleberry Finn. He headed a major metropolitan Homicide squad up close and personal, eyeball to eyeball with the all-too-real styles of murder common to any big city—from the detachment of a hired hitman to the sudden retaliation of a long-abused wife to the hands-on savagery of beheaders, garroters, butchers—a bleak, grueling job that made the world seem like a slaughterhouse.

A curtain of sadness descended on Duffy's face. "Well, the Sheppard case has screwed up this trip. With my luck I'd be out in Breton Sound and the whole damn investigation would break. Shit. My weekend's gone to hell and we don't even know if Sheppard's dead."

"About St. Petersburg . . ."

"What about it?" he snapped.

"If I left tomorrow, I could be back the middle of next week."

"Leave tomorrow? What are you talking about? You want a weekend in Florida?"

"That's where the answer may be."

"Dillmann," he said. I'd been *John* a few minutes before. "We're not Interpol. We don't have unlimited personnel and resources. Look at what we've already spent."

"And will continue to spend, probably. A solid background check in Florida, the missing man's home base, could be the least expensive way to go."

"You want a trip to Florida?"

Damn. He was seeing me, margarita in hand, basking on a beach stacked with voluptuous bikini-clad beauties.

"Tom," I said. "This is business. It could be the best three hundred dollars the department ever spent."

He brought his feet down from the desk, not a good sign. "Tell you what, Dillmann. *You* march into the corner office and tell Henry that the way to solve the Sheppard case is for you to spend a weekend in Florida."

I should have. Had I gone to St. Petersburg then, I might have cracked the case before Sheppard ever turned up. Still, I wonder now if anything would have made a difference.

This Friday, the 27th, I contacted Price, met him for dinner, told him of our efforts, and again pleaded with him to hold off on that press conference and announcement of the reward. I didn't know if I could rein him in, and if we racked up a few more unsuccessful days, I probably shouldn't even try.

We argued. "John," Price said, "I'm an expert at finding missing persons, especially runaway kids. I've located them and brought them back from foreign countries, a tricky arrangement. I've even operated from the other side of the Berlin Wall. Over the last five years I've located hundreds of missing people. It's my specialty."

"Those have been mostly children," I said.

"Same thing."

"Not the same thing at all," I said, and pointed out what he already knew.

Finding a youngster requires talking to his or her companions, the parents (who often haven't kept tabs on their offspring or withhold information out of embarrassment), and then going back to the peers offering, say, a hundred dollars—more money than they've ever had in their lives—to learn the whereabouts of their friend. A cop investigating a missing-persons case doesn't have a C-note to wave around and buy information, but a p.i. does. A generous supply of ready cash insures a private detective's high success rate.

A missing adult is different. Here the detective searches for a lover, an extorted employer, or a background with suicidal tendencies, alcoholism, or a drug or gambling addiction. Almost anything. When looking for an adult, a hundred-dollar bill won't get the job done.

Missing *children* ranks as one of the few areas where a p.i. has the advantage over the police. He can offer money and spend the time needed to do a good job. Poor Ray Himel, our one-man missing-persons unit, got fifteen new missing-children files a day, and *no* reward money to spread around.

On most other cases, the p.i. struggles at a disadvantage. The cop has the power, resources, and authority of the state behind him. In some instances he can compel a witness to cooperate. This same witness can tell a p.i. to get lost.

"We don't have a missing child," I concluded to Price. "We have a disappeared adult. What's more, we both agree the case isn't a missing person at all. It's probably homicide."

"Your approach isn't accomplishing anything," he said sensibly. "Everything you say may be true, but Sheppard is still missing."

"Dick. Please. Give us a few more days. We don't want people getting the impression of a violence-ridden Bermuda Triangle-type French Quarter that swallows up tourists."

"If the shoe fits . . ."

"It doesn't. This is an anomaly."

"Okay, John. I'll wait. But just a few more days."

* * *

That weekend, January 28 and 29, I spent in the French Quarter contacting every source I had developed over more than ten years on the force. Some I went to reluctantly; my best sources could only be squeezed so many times, and I needed to use care when I did. A major fence, for example, had to be met at a remote location, lest he be seen with me.

I learned zero. There weren't even rumors. People who usually knew every coming and going in the French Quarter professed complete ignorance about the fate of the St. Petersburg doctor.

I went to the Ursulines Guest House to have a look for myself. Dr. Sheppard's room remained as the maid had left it, just as Big Hector had described. I examined every inch of the place: No murder had been committed here.

Wandering from one gay bar to another, showing Sheppard's picture, I tried to imagine what had happened to the doctor. If murder had been his fate, surely it hadn't come on these busy French Quarter streets. They (mostly) wax and wane twenty-four hours a day, but are never deserted. He had to have gone, or been taken, somewhere. Probably he went of his own volition, notwithstanding what his friends said, because an abduction would have been witnessed.

*Everything* was speculation, so I quickened my pace. With frustration feeding an obsession, I determined to call on every bar in the Quarter that had a pool table. Maybe Sheppard had stopped to shoot a game. Maybe he had picked someone up, misjudged him, and paid for it.

If so, nobody admitted remembering the doctor. I wore my shoe leather thin all day Saturday, and drew darkly disapproving glances from Diane when I headed out again Sunday morning for results that duplicated the previous day's.

* * *

Late Sunday afternoon I cut short my canvass of ratty French Quarter hangouts where Sheppard might have shot pool and took Diane, Todd, and Amy for dinner at my grandparents' home in the comfortable Lakeview section of New Orleans.

My grandfather, John Dillmann, Sr. (I'm Dillmann III), worked for Jackson Brewery for thirty years as a route driver, and my grandmother, Germaine, the matriarch of the family, is a proud, dignified lady whose gumbo and crawfish bisque rival any served in the finest New Orleans restaurants. They loved seeing their great-grandchildren, and we loved the visits.

Certainly such a precious get-together took priority over my French Quarter travels, but the clincher was Diane, who saw less and less of me. What with the homicide job and its overtime plus the detail at the Bourbon Orleans eating up almost all our family time, she had just cause to suggest that if I liked my work so much, maybe I should marry *it.*

I held Price off for one more day, hoping something would break, but my heart wasn't in it any more. NOPD's hopes of finding Sheppard had fizzled out. Maybe the St. Petersburg private eye could do better.

Price held his press conference Tuesday morning, February 1, and, as I expected, he was every ounce the showman. This was no rumpled Philip Marlowe looking grubby and discombobulated after a seven-day bender. Price had his act together, a modern super sleuth, impeccably dressed, diamonds glistening. Representatives of the press could tell that here stood Mr. Late-Twentieth Century, with class-act secretaries managing a computer-powered office, able to cut with a surgeon's precision to the heart of a case. They had to love this quotable, colorful, chic p.i. who conducted his press conference at the Marriott. I watched him later on the noon news, and decided to steer a wide course around any place Henry Morris might be.

The afternoon edition of the *States-Item,* the P.M. version of its better-known sister, the *Times-Picayune,* featured Price on page one (most murders never make page one) in a story guaranteed to provide NOPD with an abundance of Maalox moments:

> A $10,000 reward is being offered for information leading to the finding of Dr. Mark Sheppard, a millionaire St. Petersburg, Fla., physician and art collector who has been missing here since Jan. 19 . . .
>
> Price distributed reward bulletins today to restaurants, bars, and pool halls in the French Quarter, where Sheppard is believed to have gone on his frequent trips to New Orleans.
>
> Sheppard, a 50-year-old collector of Rolls-Royce automobiles, checked into the Ursulines Guest House, 708 Ursulines St., on Jan. 19.
>
> The doctor had been seen that afternoon playing pool at Cigar's Pool Hall, 132 Exchange Place.
>
> He was reported missing on the morning of Jan. 23 when he failed to report to a St. Petersburg hospital where he was to assist in several operations.
>
> The Pinellas County Circuit Court in St. Petersburg declared Sheppard legally missing earlier this week and appointed Betty Woodard, a long-time neighbor and friend, conservator of his estate. At the same time, the court authorized the posting of the reward money.
>
> Price, a former Florida legislator, said that Sheppard lives in a $300,000 home, has four Rolls-Royces in his garage, and is worth more than $1 million.
>
> The investigator said any information about the missing doctor should be telephoned collect to his detective agency, the Nationwide Bureau of Investigation, in St. Petersburg.

> He also said he will be staying at the Marriott Hotel through Saturday and can be contacted there.

Price handed out reward posters while the cameras whirred, a politician's friendly smile on his face. What would make Henry Morris blow a gasket, I suspected, was that the reward poster urged everyone, even "highway patrol departments, police departments, sheriff's departments, and federal law enforcement agencies," to contact *Price.*

Every nightmare Morris had about the private investigator materialized in that reward poster. Though he didn't mean it this way, Price might as well have said, "In your face, Henry. I'll show you real police work. I'll accomplish what an army of your guys couldn't."

I caught up with Price at Cigar's. He was passing out reward circulars. "I'm gonna collect that money," one customer told him.

"Good for you," Price said. "Do you know where the doctor is?"

"I got the contacts to find out. I know everybody in the Quarter. That ten thousand is as good as mine."

"I hope you're right."

"Right as rain. I know everybody. Listen, I'll need some bread to get around. How about an advance on that reward, since you're sure to owe it to me anyway?"

I had to laugh. Price was perceived as holding all the aces, and here he stood, attempting to disengage a derelict's grip from his expensive sports jacket.

Still, the mere chance that he might solve the case on our turf had already stirred all of Homicide. Murder detectives sensed this and some of them, who hadn't made particularly strong efforts in the past, were out zealously beating the bushes, leaning on their informants, calling in favors carefully preserved over years.

In light of this, I believed, wrongly, there would now be no objections to my going to St. Petersburg. Hell, I thought, Chief Morris might personally strap me into a seat. It was an attractive proposition: Perhaps I could venture onto *Price's turf* and solve the disappearance.

One part of the reward poster troubled me: The payoff for Sheppard *alive* was $10,000; if dead, "Smaller amounts of the reward will be paid for information leading to the location" of the body. I asked myself, what motivated offering money for a deceased Dr. Sheppard? Did the reason involve the will? If Sheppard's body were never found, he couldn't be declared dead for seven years, a long time to wait for the estate to be carved up. Wouldn't the heirs want that body found? I knew of no individual who had killed for insurance money or a share of an estate who was willing to wait *seven years.* Such homicides get committed to satisfy an immediate need for cash. On the other hand, the heirs might not want to appear overeager, so they offered less for the corpse.

Price had said he would be fielding phone messages at the Marriott, and we walked over there together from Cigar's. I told him I might soon be in St. Petersburg conducting an extensive background investigation on Dr. Sheppard, and he again seemed pleased by the prospect.

"What about Doctor Sheppard's telephone records?" I asked.

"I'll express them to you as soon as I get back to St. Pete."

"How about his will? Have you obtained a copy?"

"I'll talk to Joe Bradham, but I want to do it in person. I don't think it will be a problem."

"Dick, you realize, don't you, that the department isn't happy about that flier?"

"Why?" He seemed surprised.

"Because you're offering a reward and asking that information be sent to you in St. Pete. But this may be a New Orleans crime."

"Christ, John, I'm being paid to find Doctor Sheppard. If there's been a crime and I receive information, you'll be the first to know."

I liked hearing this.

"Remember our first meeting?" Price asked. "I said I wanted to work *with* you. I was serious."

I didn't doubt him. I gave him my number at the Bourbon Orleans and my home phone. When I left him that evening, I still believed he and NOPD could coexist, but I *knew* I couldn't persuade my superiors that they should trust him.

What followed I call the Great Poster War. The department covered the city with fliers about the missing doctor and ours advantageously featured Sheppard's face. Of course, we overwhelmed Price in the manpower field, and even in the area of media influence. We contacted all branches of the news media, furnishing them photographs and asking them to urge anyone with information to contact Homicide.

Where Price—if he really was the enemy, as much of the department viewed him—held the clear advantage was his prominently displayed $10,000 reward offer. Money talks. An informant could collect whether he came to us or Price, but most people didn't know that.

I renewed my St. Petersburg trip discussion with Tom Duffy. He thought it was a good idea, but it got torpedoed by the fact that despite all the publicity, we still had nothing more than a missing-persons case. What if Sheppard miraculously stumbled out of nowhere suffering from amnesia? NOPD had already spent a fortune on the investigation, and a Florida trip paid for by a department perennially short of funds might seem extravagant down the road.

* * *

Price arrived back in St. Pete late on Saturday night, February 5, and was on the phone to me early the next morning.

"What you got?" I asked.

"A possible informant in New Orleans. A cabbie, name of Floyd Reeves."

"What did Floyd tell you?"

"I didn't talk with him. He called St. Anthony's and left a rather lengthy message. I figured I should pass it on."

"Shoot."

"Reeves said that on January 22—a Sunday—he picked up a man he's sure is Sheppard at the corner of Canal and Royal. The guy wanted to go to the airport, but first he had Reeves stop at a gas station so he could pick up a map. After he studied the map he offered Reeves fifty dollars to drive him to a small hospital near Baton Rouge. That's what the cabdriver did."

"What else?"

"That's it."

"You didn't call Reeves?"

"I figured you'd want to do that." He gave me the phone number.

"May I speak with Floyd?" I said, after I'd hung up with Price and dialed the number he'd provided.

"You got him." The voice was high-pitched, almost a whistle.

"My name is John Dillmann. I'm a New Orleans police department detective working on the Mark Sheppard disappearance. I . . ."

"*Detective* Dillmann? You're a cop? How'd you get my name?"

"From St. Anthony's Hospital in St. Petersburg. You called there, didn't you?"

"Sure I did. But I wanted to talk to the private investigator. The one with the money. You guys got no money, 'less you steal it."

I didn't think I was going to get along with Floyd Reeves.

"Look, Floyd, Dick Price—that's the private investigator—is working with the police department. If you have something coming, I'll make sure you get it."

"I know where this doctor is, but I want to talk to Dick Price. That's why I called him, not you. I wasn't born yesterday. Price is the one with the checkbook."

"What do you do, Floyd?" He had succeeded in getting on my nerves. His voice resembled a pre-teen's headed into adolescence, though I suspected he was in his fifties. Well, I'd have to put up with him if he could lead us to Sheppard. "How do I even know you're legit?" I said.

"I'm legit, all right. You better believe it. I'm a cabdriver. Have the money guy, Price, call me."

"Price is in St. Petersburg. You and I are here. Let's get this shit over with. Tell me what you know. If you're straight and we find the doctor, you get the money. You have my word."

"Uh-uh. I talk to the guy with the cash."

I didn't need this. To hell with the job, I thought. I cooled off, however, called Price, and he said he'd contact the cabdriver, set up a meet, and be back in touch with me.

Which he was, a half hour later, saying he would fly in late this night. He said the cabbie would meet the plane, and I should, too.

"What did Reeves tell you?" I asked.

"Just that he was sure he had Sheppard in his cab. That he could take me to the hospital where he dropped him off. He says he'll drive us to Baton Rouge."

"*I'll* drive us to Baton Rouge."

I brought Fred Dantagnan with me to the airport. Most people just take a look at Fred and start talking.

New Orleans International was virtually deserted at midnight, and so was the gate where Price's flight was scheduled to arrive. Since only one other individual awaited the plane's arrival—he stood 5′3″ and weighed about 230, wore baggy pants, a checkered shirt, and be-bop cap—Fred and I figured we had spotted Floyd Reeves. I had agreed not to approach him until Price debarked the plane and introduced himself.

Predictably, Fred didn't like this arrangement at all. He had grumbled all the way out to the airport, and now I figured he wouldn't honor the agreement to wait. "You know," he said, "Price didn't have to make this trip."

"How's that, Fred?"

"We could have cross-checked the phone number, gotten his address, and gone out to see him."

"He said he'd only talk to Price."

"Huh. He'd talk to me."

Yes.

Fred started mumbling again, and scruffing the tile with the soles of his shoes. I'm sure he thought of all the countless hours we had wasted on fruitless pursuits. Every so often he shot murderous glances at our cabbie—a paunchy guy puffing a cigar and munching potato chips.

Price's plane duly set down, and we allowed him a few lines of dialog with Reeves before making our own introductions.

"You didn't say anything about the police," Reeves squeaked at Price.

*Take it easy,* I thought, trying to aim telepathy at Fred. I knew he had no patience for this situation. It was a police matter, and two detectives were on hold because this guy in a be-bop hat thought we'd steal his reward. Maybe it wouldn't be so bad if Fred exploded. We'd hear Reeves's story real fast.

* * *

I drove. Fred sat next to me. Price and Reeves were in the backseat. I waited until we were on I-10 heading west, then flipped on the interior light and handed a picture of Sheppard over my shoulder. "Floyd," I said, "take a look at this. Is this the man you drove to the hospital?"

"That's him. He didn't say he was a doctor, but that's the guy."

"What kind of hospital is this?" Price asked.

"I don't know. He pointed out this little house, and that's where I dropped him off."

"House," Fred snorted.

"I thought you said hospital," I said.

"It was a house on the grounds of a hospital."

"Did he look sick?" Price said.

"No. He was just real quiet."

"Did he carry any luggage?"

"No. That's what I found strange. First he wants to go to the airport, then to this hospital, and he don't even have a bag."

Reeves directed us to the little town of Carrville, and then to the United States Public Service Hospital, a big place I'd never known existed. We drove through a large gate and for several hundred more yards until Reeves told us to stop in front of a small white frame house. There was no sign of life, although by now it was almost three in the morning.

"This is where he got off," Reeves said.

I drove back to the gate and talked to a guard. He said the person in charge at this hour was Dr. Lydia Zaunbrecher, and we asked him to contact her, wake her up if necessary, that we were homicide detectives from New Orleans.

Maybe it was the mood of this place, in the middle of nowhere, spooky, at least at night—an atmosphere movie producers might find perfect for a film about government scientists conducting mad experiments, or outer-space aliens establishing a base of operations—but somehow it struck me as an appropriate spot to solve the mystery of the disappeared doctor. Probably because I couldn't see very well at night, these isolated grounds reminded of a vaguely recalled Grade B sci-fi flick from my childhood, I felt a sudden surge of hope. My reaction previously had mirrored Fred's: Floyd Reeves was a crackpot, a stubborn, greedy nut, and having to follow leads like this constituted a major downside of our job.

The guard reached Dr. Zaunbrecher, who told us to come straight to the hospital, a good-sized building, it turned out. The three of us went inside, leaving Reeves to wait in the backseat hoping we threw a seven. The feisty cabbie raised a fuss about being abandoned at "the moment of truth," but we felt we looked weird enough without him.

"Screw that guy," Fred decided. "I almost hope Sheppard isn't here. That way he won't get a reward."

Dr. Zaunbrecher—aptly named for my imagined movie—looked as if we had awakened her. She was in her early thirties, attractive, dressed in a medical frock.

I showed her Dr. Sheppard's picture and she didn't recognize him. She checked the patient directory. "No Doctor Mark Sheppard," she said.

"Doctor," I said, "our information is that he may have visited a house on these grounds. It's a small, white, wood-frame building behind the hospital and to the right. We took a look at it before calling you."

"Right. That's Ralph Gaustaferro's residence. He's our supervisor of nurses."

"I'm sorry, but we need to wake him and talk to him."

"I think he may be working. Let me check."

It turned out Gaustaferro was on duty in the women's infirmary. Dr. Zaunbrecher led us there, and to disappointment.

Gaustaferro looked at Sheppard's picture and shook his head. "There are definite similarities," he said, "but the man you're asking about is David Down."

Down was a businessman, Gaustaferro explained, who lived in New Jersey. Gaustaferro and his wife, also a nurse, had many years before brought Down back to health from a serious illness.

The businessman never forgot. He corresponded regularly, visited when he could, even, on times like January 22, dropped in unexpectedly.

Reeves, red-hot to collect the reward, probably fantasized that Down said he was a doctor headed for St. Petersburg. The facial features, weight, and height of Sheppard and Down *were* remarkably similar. The cabdriver had made an honest mistake, but we were back at square one.

# •6•

PRICE had brought us Sheppard's bills from General Telephone Company of Florida (but not his will—attorney Bradham wasn't sure he should turn it over to us). After getting the p.i. on a return flight to St. Petersburg, I drew up a master list of all calls the doctor had made to and from New Orleans—some thirty different numbers—and checked them with the Blue Book, a cross-index matching listed phone numbers with addresses. To obtain locations for the unlisted numbers not printed in the Blue Book, I called South Central Bell's security office, stated my reasons for needing the information, and was informed it would take a day.

On February 7, after obtaining names and addresses for the thirty-odd numbers, I automatically scratched off a few of them: Ursulines Guest House, John T's restaurant, Ponce Woods, Larry Cephas.

I visited Hudson Real Estate and learned Sheppard had been negotiating to buy the Ursulines Guest House, located on some of the most expensive property in the city.

At a New Orleans doctor's office, I found out (1) Sheppard had graduated from LSU Medical School twenty years earlier, and (2) the doctor I interviewed had been a med school classmate of his. There had been nothing even mildly controversial about Sheppard: He hadn't drawn attention to himself, hadn't been the class clown, nothing, just a serious student with good grades and a lucrative career ahead of him.

I made a third stop to see an art-and-antique dealer doing business out of a large ante-bellum home on Esplanade. This individual told me he had been instrumental in arranging the gift of the Jackson bust to what I discovered was the New Orleans Museum of Art. He had been selling Sheppard antiques and paintings for more than ten years. The doctor was a good businessman, he said, knew what he wanted, and how much he should pay for it.

On February 7 and 8 my phone-call trackdown netted a former lover and a variety of businesses (including Adler's, an exclusive jewelry store)—all of which seemed unconnected to his disappearance. Like everything else we had tried in the search for Dr. Sheppard, this too added up to zero. Frustration, bordering on hopelessness, began to set in for me and the other homicide detectives who ran down leads on our own time.

With so many people working the case, a clearer picture of the missing man began to emerge, and I constructed a disjointed profile using what we'd learned about him.

Acquaintances considered Mark Sheppard an individual of contrasts, describing him variously as "upper-upper-crust" or as "a very low-class person"—nothing in between. When playing the elite role, he frequented places like the Royal Orleans, Commander's Palace, Brennan's; he exhibited the "low-class" part of his personality at Cigar's and Molly's, picking up men—straight, bisexual, gay. The straight males he always paid, and some of the others, also.

Sheppard did not drink or gamble heavily. In New Orleans he traveled exclusively by taxi (in St. Pete he had a chauffeur), took few chances, and maintained extreme caution toward pickup lovers. Still, this was a dangerous way to live. The most cunning con men, and even stone-cold killers, can charm the socks off their victims.

Sheppard had never married. Many years before he had been bisexual, gradually became homosexual, then refined his preferences further to young, muscular black males.

No one could remember his ever having stayed out after midnight.

None thought him suicidal.

Colleagues talked of his dedication to his profession, his marvelous skills as a doctor, but considered him a self-centered loner.

A pattern emerged with Sheppard's lovers. While virtually all of them talked about him as a "nice person," "highly intelligent," a "man of culture," none professed a deep attachment. At the time I thought perhaps he wanted it this way, a series of pleasure-grabbing flings, but later I came to believe he really did seek something permanent. Most of the lovers admitted to trying to obtain money from Sheppard, over and above the charge for quick sex. They invented heart-rending problems that a substantial injection of cash could solve. Almost always Sheppard would give them $100 or $200, but not anywhere near what they asked.

On February 12 Malcolm Cherimi, a detective sergeant in robbery, received a telephone call that shook the department. The body of Mark Sheppard may have been found.

The call Cherimi took came from a LaPlace (thirty miles southwest of New Orleans) sheriff's captain who told him a corpse had been discovered in a local junkyard at 8:00 A.M. that day. The body had been burned in half, but identification might still be possible. The captain had received our teletype messages, and the height and estimated weight of the burn victim matched Sheppard's. He then read Cherimi the teletype he was about to send out over the NCIC network:

> FROM: ST. JOHN SHERIFF'S OFFICE
> TO: ALL OFFICES & STATIONS
> ITEM # 2-345-78
>
> THE PARTIALLY BURNED BODY OF UNKNOWN W/M LOCATED WOODED AREA APRPOXIMATELY HALF MILE ON DIRT ROAD PROXIMITY I-10 & I-55. BODY DESCRIPTION: W/M, 5'11", 160–170 LBS., 45–55 YOA. SUBJECT WEARING WHITE V-NECK UNDERSHIRT & JOCKEY BRAND BRIEFS & BLACK NYLON SOCKS. VICTIM WORE NO JEWELRY. HAD NO TATTOOS. COULD POSSIBLY BEEN CLAD IN DARK COLORED POLYESTER SLACKS WHICH APPARENTLY MELTED W/INTENSE HEAT THAT BURNED AWAY MIDSECTION OF VICTIM'S BODY. ACTUAL CAUSE OF DEATH UNKNOWN FROM PRELIMINARY POST MORTEM EXAM. FINGERPRINTS, BLOOD TYPE & DENTAL IMPRESSIONS ARE TO BE MADE AVAILABLE 2/13/78.
>
> ALL S.O. & CITY P.D. REQUESTED CHECK RECENT MISSING FILES FOR POSSIBLE ID TO VICTIM.

At 1:00 P.M. Dantagnan and I walked the single block from Homicide to the Orleans Parish Coroner's Office where the body had been transferred, since St. John Parish had no facilities to perform an autopsy or store a corpse.

I always enjoyed walking with Fred, especially on cold days. He wore a heavy coat that made him seem six feet wide, and startled pedestrians seeing him coming on the sidewalk hurried to get out of the way. Watching him bowl along, however, wasn't as amusing as his "knock" when we went to the house or apartment of an individual we wanted to question. *BLAM! BLAM! BLAM!* Dantagnan's powerful fist would pound, rattling the hinges. If anyone was home, I could count on wide, worried eyes peeking out a window at this bear, and the occupant refusing to come to the door. Fred didn't mean to scare anyone; it never occurred to him that he did. Anyway, he and I had taken this walk to the coroner's office many times before. He enjoyed looking at bodies. I'd gotten used to it.

The corpse was pulled out of the refrigerated storage unit and Dantagnan moved closer to get a better view. The body was totally black, charred, permanently twisted into the shape of a monster—a Crispy Critter, according to the gallows humor that kept Homicide cops able to live with the unspeakable. The burn pattern clearly indicated the mid-section of this body had been saturated with a flammable liquid and the fire spread from there. It had been burned in two, and still held the sickly sweet smell of charred flesh, the most disgusting odor I've ever encountered.

Was this what remained of Mark Sheppard? I couldn't tell, and neither could Fred, who eyeballed parts of the body from as close as four inches.

The physical description fit. The thought occurred that the victim had been alive when set afire, the body was so contorted.

Fred and I visited the office of Coroner Franklin Minyard, one of the best known, trusted, and respected men in New Orleans. Minyard, a detective in the true sense of the word, had on numerous occasions ensured the convictions of killers with his uncanny ability to pinpoint not only the time of death, but the exact manner in which it took place. Nothing eluded this medical Sherlock Holmes. And, besides enjoying a national reputation as an outstanding forensic scientist, he earned the nickname of Dr. Jazz in the Crescent City. A tremendously gifted trumpet player, he often appeared with the Olympic Brass Band, Pete Fountain, and Al Hirt. Whatever civic cause an organization championed, it wanted "Doc" atop its list of sponsors.

"To what do I owe the pleasure of this rare visit?" Minyard asked. He saw us all the time.

"You've got a real bad body downstairs," I said. "It came in from LaPlace. A dump job that was burned."

"Another John Doe, huh?"

"This one may be special. It could be our missing doctor from St. Petersburg."

"The description fit?"

"Same height and weight."

"Did we take prints yet?"

"No," Dantagnan said. "And the hands look pretty bad. The skin is burned off."

"We can save the fingers," Minyard said. "If we have to, we'll send them to Washington. The FBI can get prints even with the first layer of skin burned off."

"How long will that take?" I asked.

"Months maybe. Depends on how badly the body is charred."

"Can't we . . ."

"Yes, there's a faster way."

"The teeth."

"If we can obtain Sheppard's dental records," Minyard said, "I know someone who may help us. A friend of mine, Doctor Ronald Carr, one of the best dental pathologists in the country. He teaches at Tulane."

"I can get the dental records," I said.

"Do that," Minyard said. "I'll have my people save the upper and lower jawbones. Call me when you have the records. The autopsy is tomorrow morning."

A Minyard associate—Dr. McGarry or Dr. Samuels—would determine the cause of death, critical to us if the body were Sheppard's.

*Us?* I thought about Pascal Saladino. No matter the identity, the case belonged to St. John Parish.

I called Dick Price in St. Petersburg, told him what I needed, and he said, "No problem."

"Dick," I said. "Seriously. We need those charts tomorrow."

"No problem. You'll have them."

"Dick . . ."

"No problem, John. I'll get back to you this evening."

He really meant it. Price flew into New Orleans that night and I met him at the Ramada Inn on Tulane Avenue near police headquarters. Performing in what I would later learn was typical Dick Price fashion, he handed me a full set of *molded dental impressions* and said, "This is an exact replica of Sheppard's mouth two months ago, made by Doctor Nicolas Maragos, his dentist in St. Pete."

"Great," I said. "All I asked for were charts."

Price smiled proudly. Maybe that super-powered resumé of his was mostly beef.

"Any luck with the will?"

"I think Bradham will cut it loose."

"I *know* he will. He should just do it, and save us the legal hassle."

The next day Fred and I took the molds to Dr. Carr at Tulane Medical Center, and nervously paced for ninety minutes while he compared them to the jawbones the morgue had sent over. I knew much of Homicide waited just as impatiently back at Headquarters.

Dr. Carr called us into his office. He handed me a dental chart comparing Sheppard's impressions against the teeth of John Doe. As Fred and I ignorantly stared at what might as well have been a sample of hieroglyphics from Cleopatra's tomb, and politely feigned comprehension of the learned pathologist's professorial drone about incisors, bicuspids, occlusion and molar pulpotomy, my head began to spin.

Jumping into a silence I hoped signified the end and not a pause in his mini-lecture, I said, "Doctor Carr, is John Doe Sheppard?"

"Haven't you been listening? No. Positively not. There's not a single similarity."

I guess I should have been grateful that the informed no longer killed the bearer of bad news, but each time I related this negative finding, I came away feeling it was somehow *my fault* that Doe wasn't Sheppard. Telling Duffy ranked the hardest, because I knew he had to report to Morris. Nor did I win any kudos when I called LaPlace and told the police captain that St. John Parish had an unidentified murder-victim investigation to handle. Nuts to them, I thought; at least they had a dump site to work with, and a body.

Not that any of us had time to worry. The Great Poster War produced literally hundreds of leads, and all of them, except the most obviously ludicrous, had to be followed up. My allotment of tips to sift through included a taxi driver who claimed Sheppard was one of his fares the night of January 19. I verified he had driven the doctor to John T's, but this information neither helped the investigation nor qualified the ambitious cabbie for the $10,000 reward. And a barber who thought he had given Dr. Sheppard a haircut on January *21*—clearly a matter of mistaken identity. And a police officer with a French Quarter beat, John Reilly, passed along the name of an informant who supposedly knew who had killed Dr. Sheppard, but the "killer" himself had been murdered. This nightmare boiled down to the snitch being what cops call a "roach," a nut, a publicity seeker manufacturing information. The individual "murdering" Sheppard hadn't existed, much less been killed himself, but reaching these conclusions forced me into that most tedious of exercises, proving a negative.

Droves of psychics came out of the woodwork for the Sheppard case, an event thoroughly anticipated in Chief Morris's attempt to keep the investigation low-key. Although I know a detective who swears a psychic nailed one of his cases right on the head, they have never helped me. I couldn't get worked up by a "vision" of a dump site near water and trees. What place, I asked, wouldn't have water and trees, especially in south Louisiana. I suspected psychics had nothing to lose from passing on information and that their motivation centered on the chance to press a reward claim if they had guessed correctly.

One lead I did get enthusiastic about. The owner of a bar catering to low-income patrons in a part of New Orleans called Girt Town phoned to say that one of his customers—known by the nickname "Baby"—had been bragging about robbing white tourists in the French Quarter. The ghetto-bar owner described Baby as 6′2″, 185 pounds, possessing "a mean temper, the kind of guy who will hurt you. I heard Baby talking about a rich doctor he had stolen a lot of money from."

This fit the scenario I imagined. Baby, who owned an automobile, could have grabbed Sheppard, stuffed him into his car, and driven to a remote area where he robbed and killed him. The bartender's story had a ring of authenticity and I *sensed* I might have come across the genuine article.

I took Fred with me, of course. We strode into the Fern Street bar as if we belonged there, *looking like police*—suits, ties, overcoats, two white guys who *had* to be cops. This way we had a shot at avoiding the trouble we'd encounter as civilians.

Every set of eyes locked onto us, the hatred palpable. We weren't just unwanted here, but actively despised. In the dim light, we scanned a torn pool table, a 1940s juke box, pinball machines, and maybe ten customers, mostly young black toughs. I asked the bartender about Baby, and he nodded toward a tall man standing alone at the end of the bar.

"You Baby?" I asked.

He looked from me to Dantagnan, lingering longer on Fred. "Oh, man, shit, what now?"

"You got some ID?" Fred asked. "Let's see it."

Everyone in the bar had drifted a little farther away, giving themselves room. The place had grown eerily quiet, the air heavy, the way it feels just before a hurricane tears in from the Gulf.

The expired driver's license said we talked to Jerome Gupton.

"Jerome," I said, "why are you called Baby?"

"The women say I have a baby face."

"Where do you stay?"

"Back of town on Annunciation Street." This was like my saying "in Slidell." "Back of town" meant the St. Thomas Project.

"You wanted?" Fred asked.

"Wanted? I just rolled out of parish." Parish Prison was across the street from police headquarters.

"You out on bond?"

"No. The D.A. dropped the charges. Look, man, can't we go on the sidewalk? I don't like these dudes knowing my business."

That suited us fine. We went outside, ignoring sullen,

hostile stares, spread-eagled Gupton against the wall of the bar, and patted him down.

"I'm clean, man," he protested. "I'm not holding." Not carrying a weapon.

Fred got his clipboard and jotted down some information to run in the computer.

"You work?" I asked.

"Yeah. I'm a longshoreman. I work when there's work."

As I continued to chat with our suspect, Fred called the background into Headquarters on the radio in our plainclothes unit. In less than a minute he came back with the verdict: "He's clean. Like he told us, he just rolled out."

Gupton had been busted on January 18, which made him innocent. We started back toward the car, and he called to us, "Man, why'd you hassle me?"

I turned around, unable to resist. "Sorry, Jerome," I said. "We just had the wrong Baby."

So it went, February 14 and 15, pulling the Bourbon Orleans security detail, working my own cases on the graveyard shift, following leads on the Sheppard investigation. It became clear enough for even the blind to see that, without a crime scene or a body, we chased a phantom, a puff of smoke we would never lay our hands on.

On the morning of February 15, as I drove toward home after graveyard ended, stomach and chest pains literally bent me over. It had started four hours earlier, went away, came back like a hard jab to the belly, abated, then returned with renewed fury. Now, on my way to Slidell, the sharp stabs attacked with increased constancy and severity. I thought it was a heart attack—it felt like an elephant was standing on my chest.

I turned the car around and went to the office of my doctor, Arnold Alper, in midtown New Orleans. He wasn't in, but his nurse reached him, described my symptoms, and he said to head for the emergency room at Mercy Hospital, where he'd meet me.

I made it—barely. The pain was terrific, but the fear was worse. I thought I might die. An emergency room doctor gave me a nitroglycerine capsule, ran an EKG, and then Dr. Alper arrived to read it.

"I don't think it's your heart, John," he said. "But I'm admitting you right away for tests and observation."

After they finished the preliminary poking and prodding and situated me in a room, I called home and told Diane rather sheepishly what had happened. She, bless her heart, didn't say "I told you so." But she had, and in their round-about way, so had Fred and Pascal.

Fred visited at the hospital. What did you expect? was his attitude, a pretty good one, I suspect. He acted disgusted when I asked him to keep me abreast on any news of Sheppard, but I believed he would. He knew not knowing would cause more worry than periodic updates.

Two days later I learned I had an ulcer at the entrance to my stomach. Dr. Alper said the pain precisely mimicked a heart attack. "John," he said, the morning of February 17, "I'll let you go home in a few days, provided you take it easy. If you don't this will turn into something very serious. You're killing yourself with coffee, cigarettes, and stress."

"It comes with the territory, Doc," I said.

"I realize you have a stressful job," he said, "but you're adding to the problem by the way you approach it. I'm putting you on a strict diet, and you're to take off work for at least thirty days to give this a chance to heal. An ulcer is like an open wound *inside* your body. If you don't take precautions, it will fester and bleed. Then you'll be in real trouble."

I was ready for the program. I told myself, by God, thirty

days sounded good to me. I had accrued enough sick leave so the city would have to pay for my time off.

For all of an hour I imagined the joy of reacquainting myself with Diane and the children, of leisure reading and watching TV and quiet drives in the country—then the phone rang.

# •7•

"SHEPPARD's body turned up," the unemotional voice over the telephone told me. It belonged to veteran Desk Sergeant Fred Turlein.

"Where?" I sat upright on the bed.

"Off of Almonaster. It looks like a dump job. The body's bad."

The Inter-Coastal Waterway runs near Almonaster, permitting ships access to area industrial plants without having to travel up the Mississippi River from the Gulf of Mexico. A big time saver. I shuddered thinking about this dreary, forbidding spot in eastern New Orleans, near the city landfill, a rural, swampy, hellish den of giant rats, snakes, alligators, and fat, slimy leeches.

"Who's handling the scene?"

"Dantagnan. But most everyone is out there."

"Are they sure it's Sheppard?"

"Yeah. Fred wanted you to know. He said to tell you everything's under control, for you to go home. He'll call you with an update."

Having been involved in the debilitating, mark-time search for Sheppard—a month that seemed forever—I had come to consider the case my own. Indeed, I had done a lion's share of the work, and now couldn't resist the temptation of visiting the crime scene. I knew Dantagnan would do an excellent job, but if the case became officially mine, which I suspected had been Duffy's master plan, I needed to study things for myself. It's similar to missing a good movie. No matter how detailed, a second-hand description can never capture the essence of the drama. Also, while Dantagnan might spot something I would miss, the opposite could also be true.

I got dressed and nobody noticed me leaving the hospital. *Hell, just stay calm. See what you can, don't get stressed, make sure the blood pressure doesn't rise. You've worked hundreds of crime scenes. This will be as relaxing as a Sunday afternoon stroll through the Garden District.*

Almonaster "Avenue" is a misnomer for a lonely, two-lane stretch of concrete bisecting a swamp. Out here the balmy breezes off the Gulf mix the unpleasant odor of stagnant water with the putrid smell of the Crescent City's only garbage dump to create a memorable stench, more lasting than any stockyard's. Picture a creature risen from the Black Lagoon stumbling along a disused, potholed road built through a vile swamp, and the image of where Dr. Sheppard's body was found should be clear.

When I arrived at 12:30 P.M., I had to park a hundred feet from the scene, Almonaster had become so congested. Sergeant Turlein was right when he told me, "Everyone is out there." Commander Duffy—who rarely visited the site of a crime any more—and Chief Morris himself, responding in grunts and grumbles to people who questioned him, which at the moment were a pair of newsmen from channels Four and Six. In total there were ten police cars, marked and unmarked, and two TV vans.

Finding a body out here was not unusual. A literal wasteland, consisting of everything the citizenry trashed, from dirty diapers to worn-out refrigerators, this section of New Orleans might as well also have been designated a boneyard for murder victims. At night, when it is pitch dark and as deserted as a country cemetery, a killer can cruise leisurely along Almonaster, secure that he won't encounter bothersome witnesses who might see him toss a corpse to the ever-hungry denizens of the swamp.

Everyone stood in a cluster of curiosity on the road's edge, peering down a slight incline to where Dantagnan waded ankle deep in muddy ditchwater near a partially submerged body.

"Dillmann," Duffy said, "what the hell you doing here? I thought you were sick."

"I'm all right. Are you sure it's the doctor?"

"It's gotta be. We found this in the left front pocket of those trousers you see floating down there."

Duffy handed me a plastic evidence bag containing a BankAmericard stamped in the name of Mark Sheppard. The pants hadn't been moved. Nothing had. Everything needed to be photographed just as it was found. I knew Fred had lifted that credit card very gingerly from Sheppard's pants.

"Who found him?" I asked.

"Louie Lesage. He was on patrol when this old woman flagged him down. She discovered the body just before Louie came by."

"What was a woman doing out here?"

"She's a bag lady. Collects junk to resell. She was looking for old lumber. Hell, you can find just about anything in this place." He hesitated. "Even Sheppard."

"Yeah," I said, and started down the embankment. My arm-waving balancing act during the slippery descent caught Fred's attention. He looked up at me, shook his head, his face a picture of pure disgust.

"Boy, Dillmann," he said, "you are hardheaded."

I didn't want him fussing at me. Not in front of all these people. I felt mud oozing over my shoes and creeping up the bottom of my pants.

"Didn't Turlein tell you I had everything under control?"

"Yeah. I just stopped by for a look. I'm on my way home."

"Like hell. You know what the doctor told you."

"How bad is it?" I asked, nodding at the body, hoping to sidetrack the Mother Fred lecture he was warming up to deliver.

"Doesn't get any worse. You're here, so you might as well take a look."

I did look, and quickly glanced away. Christ, it was awful. What a contrast between what was left of Sheppard, and the polished, debonair socialite he once had been. I forced myself to look again.

Sheppard's body lay face down, with the lower portion of his torso submerged in the swamp. The carcass had obviously been here for some time. His left hand was hidden under his chest. The right arm, also bent at the elbow, was nothing but bone. Swamp animals, probably foot-long rats, had eaten away all the flesh, muscles, and blood vessels from the shoulder to the tips of his fingers.

Sheppard was clad in a white T-shirt—stretched tightly over his swollen form—and nude from the waist down. A yellow fitted bedsheet had been wrapped around his head. A blue long-sleeve man's shirt and a large green plastic trash bag rested on the embankment three feet from the doctor's head. Eleven feet from the body's skeletal right arm was the pair of men's gray slacks from which Fred had taken the credit card.

Before we could process the scene (locating, documenting, and confiscating all physical evidence), the photographer needed to do his work. Merlin Lindsey from the crime lab took some twenty pictures, putting on film from a variety of angles the entire grisly display. He also carefully measured and noted the distance of various objects from the location of the body.

Meanwhile, Fred and I conducted a nose-to-the-ground hunt for any footprints or tread marks on the shoulder of the road, or hair, cloth, fiber—anything that might link the murdered to the murderer. But this was a longshot after all this time, and we found nothing.

I stepped back a couple of yards to view the area from a different perspective. What I saw—the position of the body and clothing scattered about—indicated Sheppard had been hurriedly heaved into the swamp from the road. It was probably done by two or more people. The doctor wasn't fat, but wrestling 180 pounds of dead weight from a car and shoving it down the embankment would be a backbreaker for one person. I envisioned these "night depositors"—probably greenhorns to the murder game—acting in haste out of sheer nervousness. I doubted they had been alarmed by approaching headlights.

It seemed to me the disposal of the body had been ill-planned. Otherwise the corpse and its belongings would have been weighted and therefore totally submerged in the swamp. Had the killer thought everything out, Sheppard's body would never have been found.

Normally Lindsey dusted the entire area surrounding a body for fingerprints, but this time he had nothing to print except the credit card, and it came up clean. He tried to obtain a blood sample, but the body had reached such an advanced stage of decomposition, there was no blood to obtain.

All this completed, we confiscated the gray slacks, blue shirt, and green trash bag, which was empty. I believed the pants and shirt had fallen out when the bag was thrown down the embankment.

We worked alone—Fred, Lindsey, and I—under a cold dark sky. To steer away any rubberneckers, a lone uniformed officer remained up on the road while we slogged through muck and mire. Chief Morris, Duffy, the TV reporters, all had gone back to town, happy to leave the gory drudgery to us.

Soon the uniformed officer was joined by a coroner's investigator, Don Roig, and his driver. Standing above us on the shoulder of the road next to the "meat wagon" (a station wagon used to transport bodies), they reminded me of vultures waiting to swoop down on a corpse.

"Come on," Fred shouted up to Roig, who needed to be present to take custody of any personal effects, as opposed to physical evidence, like the credit card, which went to the crime lab in the person of Lindsey.

We peered closely at the body: no sign of a stab wound, gunshot, or any trauma. Roig flipped the body onto its back, unwrapped the yellow fitted bedsheet from around the head, and exposed a hideous froglike face, swollen to at least three times its normal size. Stuck in the mouth was a dark colored man's sock.

Sheppard's face resembled nothing human. Puffed to grotesque proportions, the inflated sphere stared at us with bulging, monsterlike, wide-open eyes.

We stared back, shivering, and within a few seconds determined the cause of death: strangulation. Wrapped around Sheppard's neck were a pair of pantyhose and a white electrical cord. That answered *how.* As for *where,* it was obvious he had not been strangled here and that the next critical objective would be to find the murder location. Probably in a place providing a power source for the cord and, unless a female impersonator delivered the fatal squeeze, a place where a woman lived. Possibilities ran through my head, but I couldn't imagine why *both* pantyhose and an electrical cord were around the neck.

Mud and slime had crept up our legs almost to our hips, filthy stuff, and we had to fight the urge to shortcut this one. We knew that getting out of this hellhole and not thoroughly doing our jobs could mean, down the line, a murderer going unpunished.

Roig cut the electrical cord and pantyhose from around the neck, being careful not to disturb the knots, and Lindsey bagged them. The way they had been tied might later provide a clue to the killer's identity.

Roig and his driver carried the corpse up the embankment and loaded it into the wagon. From here they would take it to the Orleans Parish Coroner's Office for an autopsy.

Lindsey, Fred, and I remained at the scene. We plunged our arms into the water, fingers sifting the muddy bottom in search of additional evidence. We had discarded our suit coats and rolled up our sleeves, but the murky water, stained with all manner of garbage, ruined our shirts. Grousing, cursing, ruing the way we made a living, we continued bent over in the polluted bilge, dragging our hands along the bottom. Thunder rumbled nearby, sure sign of a coming storm. We felt the first raindrop. Sharp stones scratched my fingers, and Fred cut his hand on a broken bottle. We joked about snakes and alligators, but kept a sharp eye out for them. There was nothing dignified about what we did.

Back and forth we trolled, coordinating movements so nothing within a fifteen-foot radius of where the body had been would be neglected.

"John!" Fred exclaimed. "Take a look!"

He held up a pair of black horn-rimmed glasses, which appeared identical to those Sheppard wore in the driver's license picture. We did indeed later match the glasses to the slain doctor, but what seemed important at the time was finding *something.* If glasses were there, so might other personal effects or physical evidence, and we continued our dreary search. Not until 4:30 P.M., two hours later, and with dusk not far away, did we give it up.

I felt much better after a quick shower at the Bourbon Orleans and putting on the change of clothes I kept there for just such emergencies. Then I braced myself for Part II of a Mother Fred lecture about not following doctor's orders and called Diane. But she didn't gripe at me, and I wanted to hug her. She didn't say a word about my working that crime scene, choosing instead to blame "bad luck" for Sheppard's body being found at this time.

I reached the homicide office about 7:00, just in time to catch a welcome comic-relief scene starring Pascal Saladino. Duffy had called him in early to witness Sheppard's autopsy (performed right away because of the case's importance), and Sal had decided to stick around, get a jump on his investigations by working right through the graveyard shift.

I had figured out long ago that one quality which made this detective a master at solving murder mysteries was his ability to concentrate totally on the case before him to the exclusion of all extraneous matters. He even refused to clutter his mind with memorized commonplace facts like frequently used phone numbers. "If I need one, I can look it up," he said in defense of a technique that for him worked beautifully.

When I entered the office this evening, Pascal needed to call his partner to verify a point in a report.

"What's Hank's number? What's Hank's number?" Saladino called out to anyone in earshot.

This was a designed-to-order opportunity for the jokers

on second shift. I grinned and watched from the sidelines as one of the detectives rattled off Pascal's home phone number, which he dutifully dialed. An atypical silence fell over the murder room as everyone pretended to study case reports while tuning in on Sal's conversation.

So engrossed had my one-time sponsor become that he didn't recognize his own wife's voice. "Is Hank around?" he asked.

"That you, Sal?" his wife must have said.

We watched as a look of shock spread across Pascal's face. So sure-footed when it came to a murder investigation, Sal could now only put his foot in his mouth. "What the hell are you doing at Hank's place?" he asked in a stern voice.

I don't know what she said, but a roar of laughter from his co-workers answered the question. The great detective blushed like a small boy.

I let a little time pass, then approached his desk. "Pascal, can you spare a minute?"

"No. Ain't got a minute." Translation: The heavy work load this dean of homicide carried required sixteen straight hours on his current hitch. All a shift means is that the detective has to be around and available during that time. Thus, graveyard must follow up leads the hard way, on overtime, since doors can't be knocked on at 3:00 A.M.

"Sal," I said. "It's important. It's about the Sheppard autopsy."

"Oh, yeah. Right, Skinny." Saladino called everyone Skinny. "I caught you on the tube a little while ago. You finally got to see Sheppard, huh? Pretty ugly sight, huh?"

I thought about his right arm, the bulged eyes, the face ballooned up.

"Not pretty at all," Pascal said, answering his own question. "No, sir, not even to Doctor Carr, that dentist. You should have gotten a load of his face."

"What did he find?"

"The teeth were Sheppard's."

"Who did the autopsy?"

"McGarry."

"He positively determine the cause of death?"

"Sure. Strangulation. Sheppard was choked. The hyoid bone was fractured and there was evidence of hemorrhaging around the larynx."

"So the electrical cord did the trick?"

"There's no doubt he suffocated: McGarry found signs of hemorrhaging of the right temple." Saladino smiled. "You won't have to count on ballistics in this one. You're a jump ahead of the game. How many times have we recovered the murder weapon on the body? Not often. Here the weapon's been handed to you on a silver platter. Not a gun, but an electrical cord. Who owned it? Where did it come from? Answer those questions and it's case closed."

I got a good night's sleep, then started bright and early on the 18th. Diane didn't say a word. She knew, I believe, that *real stress* for me would be doing nothing, stewing, worrying about what *was* being done.

I returned to the Ursulines Guest House, talked to manager Jim Owens, and learned the hostelry used only flat bedsheets. I looked for but didn't find any small appliances from which the electrical cord could have been torn. I even went to the company that did laundry service for the Ursulines to make sure the guest house *never* used fitted bedsheets.

Back at Headquarters, I called on Charles Folmer, affectionately called Mr. Wizard, NOPD's resident electronics expert, and asked him to examine the electrical cord. What had it been attached to? A lamp? A hair dryer?

Folmer studied the cord under a microscope. "A Kawasaki," he said, "that someone ripped from a small appliance. Just yanked it out. It appears to have been soldered to a printed circuit board."

"Anything else you can tell me?" It was important: Find the appliance, find the killer.

"I'll call some Kawasaki dealers," Folmer said, "and see if I can determine the type of gadget it came from."

Commander Duffy spotted me when I arrived at my desk, and waved me into his office. He looked more upbeat than I'd seen for a long time. Maybe, he figured, we'd solve this case after all.

"John," Duffy said, "I have an idea. Sit down and let me run it by you. The answer to this Sheppard case may be in St. Petersburg."

I lifted my eyebrows, pretending admiration. Where had I heard this before? But Duffy didn't catch my meaning, and so what? He wasn't trying to be disingenuous; it wasn't part of this Irish cop's makeup. He had just forgotten.

"Some asshole Sheppard knew," Duffy continued, "strangled the shit out of him. That's the key: someone he knew. It had to happen in a house or apartment, right? Otherwise how explain the bedsheet and the electrical cord? I guess it could have occurred in a hotel room, but I think not. A house or apartment, that's it, which means one of a million places. Right?"

"Right," I said.

"Well, that's too many. We gotta narrow it down. Keep in mind that this doctor was a very cautious individual. He didn't go just anywhere. He had to trust the perpetrator enough to put himself, unknowingly, into a life-threatening situation. But who? Who did he trust that much? That's why we need a good background investigation."

"We should go for it," I said.

"I mean a thorough background. We should know more about Mark Sheppard than Mark Sheppard knew about himself. What time did he get up in the morning? What time did he go to bed? Who did he socialize with? I want to know about his business associates. That last will and testament bothers the shit out of me. We need a copy. I want to know where every nickel is going. You understand, Dillmann? Learn his fantasies, his nightmares, the brand of toothpaste he used."

"Okay," I said. I intended to provide Duffy with all of this, and more.

"Now we've got a body," Duffy was saying. "The bullshit questions—Is he dead? Isn't he dead? Is he kidnapped? Is he on holiday?—that were giving me a gigantic headache have all been answered. This baby is yours, Dillmann. Work on it. Solve it."

"When do you want me to go?"

"Yesterday. We'll make the flight arrangements. You notify the St. Pete Police Department. Count on me. I'll get you a couple of hundred from Henry for expenses."

"Right," I said.

A couple of hundred? I supposed I should be grateful. Chief Morris once told me he thought twenty dollars a day for out-of-town living expenses was generous.

What I couldn't have imagined, however, was just how much my luck had changed, nor how deep luck would allow me to go. Later I came to believe I knew Dr. Sheppard better than I knew myself.

# 8

IN a living room not much smaller than my entire house, lounging in a highback French provincial antique chair, a glass of Chardonnay on the old cherrywood end table at my right elbow, a Persian rug on the floor beneath a high-vaulted ceiling, and a huge open fireplace above which hung a heroic portrait of Napoleon, I sat in Dr. Mark Sheppard's home at 416 Brightwater Drive and tried to imagine living alone in this mansion.

A single lamp off the kitchen entrance cast long fuzzy shadows through the adjacent rooms. I kept my eyes closed, engulfed by the sounds of silence, interrupted only by the crackling fire.

What had it been like, alone, in this huge, hacienda-style home? Why would anyone want to live alone in such a place?

I had gotten an adequate lay of the land earlier from a tour of the house and grounds conducted by Dick Price, who then left me to spend the night here. Duffy wanted to know about Sheppard? What better way than to sit in his chair, walk in his footsteps, sleep, yes, sleep in the bed he used in this magnificent cavernous structure.

* * *

Dick Price met National Airlines flight 152 that arrived on time at 9:00 A.M., February 20, at Tampa/St. Petersburg International Airport. He whisked me through baggage claim and out to his spanking-new cherry-red Corvette convertible waiting in a No Parking zone. It was a perfect riding-with-the-top-down day, warm, sun shining, soft blue sky dotted with fluffy white clouds. The *St. Petersburg Times* between the bucket seats told me the bay area would soon become a sport utopia, with spring training opening for the Cincinnati Reds and St. Louis Cardinals. As a boy I had earned pocket change selling popcorn at New Orleans Pelicans games, but the lure had been getting inside and watching the players.

"St. Pete," Price said, zipping along Interstate 4 across Tampa Bay on the Howard Frankland Bridge, "is mostly a retirement community. There's a lot of old money here, not much night life. Quiet. Reserved. The opposite of New Orleans."

"What about where Sheppard lived?"

"I'll take you there later. It's in Old Northeast, the Snell Isle part of town. Very elite. What Highland Park is for Dallas, or Shaker Heights is for Cleveland."

Our twenty-seven-mile drive from the airport ended at First Avenue North and 13th Street, St. Petersburg Police Headquarters, where Price introduced me to a friend of his in Intelligence, Sergeant Ted Kramer. I had no authority in this city, but as a professional courtesy Kramer would see that I received cooperation and assistance whenever needed.

"Sheppard's been getting a lot of ink in St. Pete," he said. "It was front page, of course, when the body was found, but it was also big news when that John Doe turned up."

"It's been played strong in New Orleans, too," I said. "My file is getting thicker every day."

"Any good leads?"

"We're looking for a friend, someone he knew and trusted."

"You think the killer's from here?"

"Too early to tell."

"Well, I hope you catch the bastard. If there's anything we can help you with—transportation, search warrants, anything at all—just give us a holler, day or night."

Price had our busy itinerary set out. I had shown him around New Orleans and he was eager to familiarize me with his own stamping grounds.

We first interviewed Cyrus Hadley, age twenty-four, Sheppard's part-time butler and chauffeur. We caught him at his residence on Harris Street.

Hadley told us he met Sheppard in a bar in 1976, went to work for him shortly thereafter, serving as a butler whenever the doctor threw special small gatherings and large parties. The chauffeur duties came later. In October 1977, Hadley had accompanied Sheppard to New Orleans on one of those getaway weekends.

"Cyrus," I said, "I understand that Doctor Sheppard was extremely cautious, almost paranoid. Would this be your assessment?"

"Definitely. The doc kept to himself. He was always afraid of being found out."

"Are you a native of St. Petersburg?"

"No. I was just passing through when I met Doc. I didn't have a job, and he helped me."

"You say chauffeur. Didn't Doctor Sheppard drive?"

"Sure. But he liked to put on airs. He had these big Rolls-Royce convertibles, all restored. God knows what they're worth. When he went out to a society function, or wanted to impress someone, he had me drive. I also kept up the cars for him."

"What about his sexual activities? I assume you're aware that he was gay."

"Oh. You know."

"Did you?"

"Yes. But I'm one of the few people who did."

Price nodded. He lived in this part of Florida, had known about the prominent doctor while he lived, and never heard a breath of scandal. And in this staid community of retirees, it would have been a scandal.

"Doctor Sheppard was a very private person," Hadley said. "He went to great pains to conceal his homosexuality. That's why he went out of town so often. He feared that someone here would learn."

"That trip you made with him to New Orleans. Did the doctor introduce you to any of his friends?"

"Only one. A guy named Sly. Doctor Sheppard shot pool with him."

"Where did you meet Sly?"

"In a pool hall. A real dump on this narrow street near Canal. I don't remember the name."

I did: Cigar's.

"While you were with Doctor Sheppard in New Orleans, did he visit anyone's home or apartment, or go off with someone in a car?"

"No. Not Doctor Sheppard."

Price said to me when we were in his car, "It's what I've told you, John. This Sheppard was a walking example of an individual living in a closet."

After lunch we spent almost four hours at St. Anthony's Hospital. We must have talked to twenty people, administrators, fellow doctors, nurses, and they all spoke of Dr. Sheppard in reverent tones one might reserve for a saint. Personally Sheppard might have been Mother Teresa; professionally, a competent, beloved Dr. Spock.

I didn't mention his sexuality, because *these people didn't know.* Their Dr. Sheppard and the murder victim in my homicide file seemed to have nothing in common.

From the hospital Price guided his sports car on a zigzag path to attorney Joe Bradham's office in downtown St. Pete, with a view of the harbor, not far from the yacht club, an area with an abundance of bright green benches where elderly people sat and talked. Inside Bradham's well-furnished office I could see airplanes taking off and landing from a small airport.

"Mr. Bradham," I said, "how long have you known Doctor Sheppard?"

"A little over a year. I was recommended to him by a friend of his. Doctor Sheppard called and asked me to represent him, specifically to revise a previous will. I drew up the will, naming Betty Woodard executrix of his estate, just a day or two before he went to New Orleans. The only change besides the new executrix was taking into account that a previous beneficiary had passed away."

"Excuse me, Mr. Bradham," I said, "but didn't Doctor Sheppard cut somebody out of his will just before the trip to New Orleans?"

"He did. But that was because the individual died."

"I'm wondering about a Doctor Cabrera."

"Oh, yes. He's in the will."

"He wasn't given more? Or less?"

"No. The bequest did not change."

Nor did the state of my investigation. Evidently this doctor's visit to New Orleans at the same time as Sheppard's had been a coincidence.

"Then there would be no motive," I asked, "because of anger or disappointment from the will?"

"That's correct. Look, I'm sorry I didn't turn this over earlier, but I'd hoped Doctor Sheppard was alive, and didn't know if he'd want me to do that. Why don't I just have my secretary make a xerox copy, and you can take it with you."

It was almost 6:00 P.M. when Price and I left Bradham. "Not much more we can do today," he said. "How about a nice dinner with Twinkle and me?"

"Sure. But I'd like to get a room first."

"You want to learn about Doctor Sheppard, don't you?"

"Yes. But I thought we were knocking off."

It was then he told me, if I wanted, I could spend the night in Sheppard's house. Betty Woodard had made the residence available to me. Of course, I wanted.

"Now this is what I call an estate," I said when we pulled into the Sheppard driveway.

"Me, too," said Price. "It sits on *three* lots. Wait till you see the inside."

Price called Twinkle on his car phone and asked her to meet us at the Wine Cellar in Redington Beach for dinner. While he made the arrangements, I whipped out a tourist pamphlet I'd grabbed at the airport and leafed through it to get my bearings. A regional map showed that Price and I had driven west over an inlet of Tampa Bay and south on a small peninsula to St. Petersburg. The brochure touted 28 miles of white beach and 361 sunny days a year to enjoy a variety of vacation activities on Florida's Pinellas Suncoast: "eight individually charming communities"—Clearwater Beach, Dunedin, Indian Rocks Beach, Madeira Beach, St. Pete Beach, St. Petersburg, Tarpon Springs, and Treasure Island—on the peninsula and neighboring keys in the Gulf of Mexico. I located Redington Beach, our destination for dinner with Twinkle, on Indian Rocks Beach.

We took just a cursory look at the inside and outside of Sheppard's house—my first impression was of a museum piled high with treasures—before driving over to Redington Beach. Price said he thought his girlfriend would enjoy seeing the place after we ate.

On the way to the restaurant, I flashed back to the day I told Price I might be coming down to do a background check on Sheppard, and how he had told me, "You'll love Twinkle."

I couldn't help it. Maybe it was because I had heard so many spiels from French Quarter strip joint barkers trying to hustle tourists into their joints, but Price's words caused me subconsciously to think of something else: "Yowza, yowza, yowza, feast your eyes on this week's headliner from the golden state of Florida, the talented, tantalizing, titillating Twinkle, yowza, yowza, yowza."

The name prompted my mind to run wildly on the wrong tangent. At the Wine Cellar I expected a bimbo and met a whiz kid. Twinkle (this is her real first name—last name Baynard), 32, a 5′7″ headturner with dark brown hair, greeted us warmly. Conversing through a great shrimp cocktail, French onion soup, and delectable rack of lamb, I understood why Price beamed whenever he mentioned this intelligent, witty woman. A real live wire, "Twinkle" befit her sparkling personality.

The three of us switched to Twinkle's car after dinner and drove to Snell Isle. This time we looked more closely at the large two-story home with its terra-cotta roof, oversized rooms, and lovely backyard swimming pool. Inside it was crammed with numerous rolled-up Persian rugs, expensive statuary and paintings, countless antiques. Beautiful items lay about with no apparent rhyme or reason. There were busts of Julius Caesar and Alexander, portraits of Churchill and Eisenhower. The place was clean, not neat, *all* the contents undoubtedly very valuable, something apparent even to my untrained eye, but stored in a haphazard manner, as one might in a warehouse. This collection of a lifetime didn't give the impression of having been cast aside; rather it seemed to be *waiting.*

After the tour, Price promised to pick me up at 9:00 A.M. and he and Twinkle left. I took a walk through each room on the main level, upstairs, and basement. Attempting to knock the chill out of myself and this "museum," I lit a fire, uncorked an arbitrarily selected bottle of the dead man's wine, and relaxed in an eighteenth-century Chippendale chair. The chair, I later learned from a story in the *Tampa Tribune,* was one of the first pieces in Sheppard's extensive antique collection, purchased in his youth with savings from a $1.50-a-week job delivering newspapers.

The fire reduced to a mound of gray ashes and the wine bottle drained, I climbed the spiral staircase to the doctor's bed in the smallest (huge by normal standards) of the five bedrooms.

The next morning the ever-present question Who Killed Mark Sheppard? hammered me awake at dawn. I shuffled downstairs, put on a pot of coffee, and planted myself at the kitchen table to peruse the last will and testament of the man in whose home I now stayed.

The first portion of the document allocated gifts of cash to eight Floridians, a woman in Connecticut, a man in Tennessee, and a cousin in North Carolina. Friend and neighbor Ida White received $50,000. So did Sally Ward, Sheppard's secretary of thirteen years. Chauffeur/butler Cyrus Hadley had been earmarked for $20,000. Shares of $10,000 each went to housekeeper Nancy Woods; Fred Williams, an operating room worker at St. Joseph's Hospital in Tampa; Samuel Rosas, business manager at St. Joseph's; Florence Justus, a cousin; and Peter Kersker, a St. Petersburg attorney and restauranteur. Shares of $5,000 were bequeathed to James Aycock of Knoxville, "who presently works for the Tennessee Road Department"; Larry Rawley of St. Petersburg; and Marion Reinhardt of Madeira Beach.

Judging from the posh furnishings in the mansion, I knew the personal belongings bequeathed in the will weren't worthless, sentimental keepsakes, the type that too often causes family squabbles and deep, slow-mending wounds when it comes time to divvy up. No way could Sheppard's treasures be categorized with the milkglass bud vase Aunt LulaBelle picked up during the Depression at the five-and-dime, or the tawdry Kewpie doll Uncle Jed won pitching horseshoes at the county fair seventy years ago.

Feeling just slightly more qualified than a chimpanzee trying to select a bargain from a Sotheby's auction catalog, I did recognize enough high-dollar trademarks—Spode and Haviland china, Steuben glass, Brucellotti Sterling—to know Sheppard wasn't giving away knickknacks he bought during a K-Mart bluelight special. Article IV of the six-page document made the following bequests:

> To Sean Porter, the grandson of I. Webster Porter, Deceased, my entire library; I. Webster Porter's correspondence to me; the Florentine Square Renaissance Desk once owned by I. Webster Porter; and the Italian four-poster green and gilt bed.
>
> To my cousin Lois D'Hooge of Oak Park, Illinois, my mahogany and cherry Grandfather's Desk; what remains of the sets of old Haviland china; and the tall Russian Candelabra, which came from my mother.
>
> To Del and Betty Woodard, the larger of the two sets of Brucellotti sterling flatware; the Steuben glass and Gold "Arctic Fisherman"; and my set of Royal Crown Derby (Japan).

To Peter Kersker, the remains of my wine cellar; and the man's Brucellotti Roman Wine Cup with a gold liner.

To Truman and Kathy McGhee, the smaller Brucellotti set of silver flatware; and my Richard Ginori China.

To Ida White, my Sir Christopher Sterling Flatware; my fine crystal; Spode Independence china; and the pair of gilt Swan Candelabra.

To Dr. Grover Austin and his wife, Margaret, my Malichite objects.

To Dr. Cornelius Franckle and his wife, Ruth, my "Eagle Kagal" carpet; and the large Porcelain Oriental Vase in the living room of my home with a dragon and rooster thereon.

To Edward H. White, his choice of any of the automobiles that I may own at the time of my death.

To Stan Brunt, my yellow gold wrist watch.

Finally, the will directed that "all the rest, remainder, and residue" of Sheppard's estate, which I understood to be a substantial fortune, should be turned over to "the Franciscan Sisters of Allegany, New York, to establish the Mark Sheppard Trust Fund." Under the management of this Catholic order of nuns, income from the trust "shall be expended to further the medical education of employees (and their children) of St. Anthony's Hospital."

I had to agree with lawyer Bradham that the will, at least on the surface, didn't provide a motive for murder. Sealing off that avenue of approach, I sadly assessed what the first twenty-four hours of my evidentiary expedition had netted: one suspect, Sly, named by Cyrus Hadley as a friend of Sheppard's. But Sly was in New Orleans.

* * *

Dick Price rang the doorbell at 9:00 A.M. on the dot, and this morning he helped me interview Sheppard's neighbors in this fashionable northeast section of St. Petersburg. All these substantial, well-to-do burghers shared a common belief that they knew the doctor, but none actually did. Few had ever attended one of Sheppard's parties, and most had never been inside his house. The parties he threw, I learned, often held at poolside, usually involved guests from an altogether different culture, guests protected from outside view by the high fence surrounding the backyard.

That afternoon, following lunch, we stopped at several beachside pool emporiums where Sheppard had honed his hobby. In an altogether different atmosphere from Cigar's, we interviewed a number of people who had played against him. He was considered a "regular guy" by many; some didn't know he was a prominent medical doctor.

This night Price bought dinner at the Lobster Pot for Twinkle and me. I told him he was too generous (he had also paid the night before), and he joked about having a lot of money—"unlike cops, I know that routine"—and produced a thousand-dollar bill that he carried, I supposed, for shock value. It was a 1928 issue, signed by Andrew Mellon, bearing the portrait of President Grover Cleveland. I had never seen such a bill, and don't expect to again.

Price asked me to visit his home. He said he had a target-shooting range in the basement. "Bet I can outshoot you," he said. I would have bet on that, too.

Instead, I asked to be taken back to the mansion. "There's got to be something there," I said. "Waiting for me. I can feel it."

Twinkle stopped in mid-bite of her dessert and looked at me oddly.

"I'm sorry," I said. "I know it sounds crazy."

"No, it doesn't," Price said. "It's called a gut hunch, and I've had a few of them."

* * *

Back on Brightwater Drive, alone, 9:30 P.M., my energy level high, I began the search. First I went through all of Sheppard's desks.

Nothing.

Next I tackled his personal effects, rifling every piece of clothing in his considerable wardrobe.

Nothing.

Downstairs I sniffed out the kitchen cupboards as keenly as Old Mother Hubbard's hungry, bone-hunting dog. In the pantry—a copious supply of liver paté, artichoke hearts, and the like—I thought, *Todd and Amy would go bonkers here: no junk food.* To keep from being driven insane by the children, Diane's grocery list always included chips and cookies to satisfy the kids, and ice cream for me. But Sheppard's was undoubtedly the pantry of an adult, a gourmet at that.

Trying my best not to disturb things, I let my fingers adroitly do the walking in drawers, chests, closets, and close spaces in the guest house and garage apartment. Their work continued inside each car parked in the garage, feeling underneath seats, into the corners of sidepockets, to the back of glove compartments.

Still no clue.

I rested in the Chippendale chair my frame fit so comfortably. Eyes closed. Muscles relaxed. I tried to divine the location of that special "something."

Whatever the mode of transport—spooky guidance from the doctor's ghost, special assistance from his avenging angel, or simple common sense and a stroke of good luck—I wound up in Sheppard's study again.

Having already checked the desk drawers on my first dry run, I made a slow pivot, evaluating the contents of the room, and stopped. "Geesus," I grumbled, facing a wall of bookshelves, "it would take a week for a team of James Michener student researchers to go through all this."

*You don't have a team* or *a week. Do you want to look like a dumbass reporting ZIP to Duffy?*

"Of course not."

*Then get in gear.*

"Right," I said, pushing twice-turned shirt sleeves above my elbows and expelling a sigh.

I reached high for the first volume on the far left side and worked slowly across the top shelf. I took each book down, fanned through it, and returned it to its original position in my exasperating search for an old letter, perhaps a receipt, or whatever was that elusive "something" I hadn't discovered.

Inching tome by tome, row by row, I made my way across the wall. Mark Sheppard's love of antiquity was shelved in his library, and much of his collection attested to the ravages of time—spines bearing disjointed titles or worn smoothly blank from hundreds of handlings.

Three-fourths of the way through, I finally started coughing. Using a book as a bookmark, so to speak, I slid the one in my hand sideways and opened a window, releasing jillions of dust particles and the stifling, musty odor of pages long unread.

I took some deep breaths, my chest swelling and exhaling great gulps of salty air. As my lungs cleared, I lingered at the window watching a light breeze tickle the fringy palms in the yard. A bright, nearly full moon hung in the sky.

Picking up where I'd left off, I plowed to the end of my current shelf, where an odd-sized, three-volume set piqued my curiosity. Like so many of the others, these bore no legible titles, but closer inspection revealed the bindings were fairly new. I pulled out the threesome, which had been positioned at eye level and within easy reach from the desk chair. I read the gold imprint on the padded red leather cover of the one on top:

S. BRUNT LTD.
Precision Engineers—Rolls-Royce Specialists
Tel. Newcastle 625215

The leather volume was stamped 1978. A second volume, similarly stamped, bore the numerals 1977. And the third: 1976. I guessed S. Brunt Ltd. was a luxury automobile dealer in London.

Well, everyone said Sheppard was a Rolls-Royce fanatic, I thought, assuming I had found his automobile maintenance logs—notations of oil changes, lube jobs, tune-ups, etc.

I cracked open one of the volumes and knew I had hit the jackpot.

# • 9 •

It's not always true that dead men tell no tales. Mark Sheppard did. And for whatever had compelled him to start keeping a personal diary the first day of 1976, I was grateful.

In preparation for a long night's read, I kindled a fire in the living room, brewed a fresh pot of strong coffee, and rustled up a snack tray. I passed on the stockpile of caviar and smoked oysters, settling on a wedge of Brie with wheat crackers.

Seated at my favorite spot in the living room, this time all the lights burning bright, I began with the first entry, January 1, 1976. As the pages turned, I learned more about Mark Sheppard than anyone could ever *want* to know.

All the people I had interviewed about the doctor had used adjectives like "precise" and "methodical" to describe him, and his diaries indicated those characteristics. He was careful to mention such things as when he woke up and when he went to bed, the exact menu of each meal, specific amounts paid and owed on purchases. Several days in succession he mulled the pros and cons of buying a car that had belonged to Constance Bennett.

Maybe he penned the daily record as part of a weight-loss program. I noticed figures at the top of each page documenting current weight, number of pushups and situps, how many miles he had run or laps he swam, plus chest and waist measurements. He obviously loved good food, and judging from descriptions of meals he ate at home, as a guest at a friend's, and in fancy restaurants, I could see why he had a weight problem. But apparently the diet and exercise regimen paid off. He started the diary at 218 pounds and was down to 175 when he died. I wondered if he put himself through the aches, pains, and self-denial because he was a health-conscious physician, or to make himself more appealing to lovers.

Although Sheppard kept meticulous tabs on his physiology, finances, work schedule, and sleep patterns, the bulk of his commentaries was purely emotional: revelations of his innermost desires, secrets, and torments. I'm sure many years as a cop dealing with the underside of society had jaded me to some extent; still, I had a real problem empathizing with a fifty-year-old man, a respected professional no less, who carried on intensely about various affairs, loves, and intrigues in the super-heated, super-earnest manner of a vacuous teenager. And clearly, some of the individuals he "loved," who "tortured" him, to whose actions he attempted to attribute deep and sincere motives, were little more than teenagers themselves.

Sheppard's worries weren't real to me. I didn't give a damn about Nathan leaving Joseph to take up with Gary (who still loved Thomas), or Drew's betrayal of Eugene by showering attention on Raymond.

Quoted out of context, portions sounded suitable for a script of "Lifestyles of the Rich and Famous." "Swam in the afternoon. Then at tea time, we were having raisin bread and toast, when Reggie called from England about adding a black combed horsehair roof and lady's companion to the Bentley." But these diaries, run in their entirety, would rack up an X rating for Robin Leach.

I knew, by reversing the sexes of some of the featured characters in Sheppard's books, I could be reading the autobiography of a rich, shallow, self-pampered heterosexual, a parody of idle English lords (at least Sheppard held a job) and spoiled American heirs (Sheppard earned his own money).

Numerous times I had to put down his journals, embarrassed for him and myself. What he did and how he felt, I knew, was *his* business. Certainly he hadn't written them for a Louisiana cop. I wondered, would he want me to keep going, hoping I would find a clue to his murderer? Or would he rather I just stop? Would what I learned about his closely guarded life pain him more than allowing his killer to go free?

It didn't matter. The decision wasn't his. I had to go on, peeling layer after layer from a man's soul. Sheppard had been killed by *someone he knew*—I believed this bone deep—and barring his coming back to life to tell me, these diaries were the most likely means of identifying his killer.

Finally, around 3:00 A.M., my eyes reddened and hurting, the diary reached the last shortened month of his life. If these journals contained the answers to his death, they most likely would deliver them now. I took a sip of coffee, a deep breath, and finally, with almost morbid fascination, I plunged into reading about the final two-plus weeks of Dr. Mark Sheppard's life.

> *Sunday 1 January 1978*
> Woke up early . . . shot pool in the afternoon. Supper with the Woodards, and home to a quiet night. Only one case in the late morning. Del agreed to get up and take me to the plane in the early morning.

If he were going to provide a clue, it would have to come soon.

> *Monday 2 January 1978*
> I kept waking up all night saying to myself I must remember to pack this or that. Finally I got up at 5 and started throwing things into my suitcase. Net result: I had far too much and lots of camera stuff. Del came at 6 and we arrived at 6:25 in time for the National one-stop (Pensacola) flight to New Orleans, which arrived at 8:30 A.M. By 9 I had my luggage. To downtown in a cold rain. Checked into the Ursulines at $22 @ day instead of the $75 demanded by the Noble Arms because of the Sugar Bowl. I put away my luggage and walked over to Esplanade and Marais and went to John Smith's apartment. He had been in bed with a sore throat—enjoyed seeing him. Then walked down to Cigar's to find that he had decided to close for the day because of the Sugar Bowl. Nothing much open for lunch so I went back home and went to bed. Up at about 6 P.M. to join Paul Fitzwater in going to see the Kari and Joseph Beasley house, 2609 Ralpiel. Lovely furniture. Jacob Smith showed us the place. A strange house with no dining room, and a kitchen on the third floor, and only one bedroom. We had a couple of glasses of white wine, then over to Paul's for hot buttered rum and a supper of leftovers from Christmas. Home late and to bed.

About halfway through this January 2 entry, the figurative lightbulb exploded in my head. How many times had I heard that Sheppard would *never* visit someone's home or apartment in New Orleans? Straight from the horse's mouth, so to speak, here was virtually incontrovertible proof that he had visited the apartment of one John Smith (Paul Fitzwater also, but Fitzwater was an old friend we'd already eliminated from the murder sweepstakes). I'd have to find this man with the stereotypical American name.

> *Tuesday 3 January 1978*
> Slight hangover, but warmer weather. Had an 11 A.M. date with George Gerault to see his work. Stopped by and saw John Smith on my walk out Esplanade. George's photographs have superb composition, he uses the full frame of a Hasselblad 2½×2½. George seems afraid of color—flat surface, pastel tones, nothing gutsy. Can draw well, reminds me of Matisse; fascinated by dwarfs, one-armed and one-legged people. We went in George's truck to the Chez Helene for a wonderful stuffed pepper—ground meat, filet gumbo flavor, and shrimp. George dropped me at Cigar's and I shot Jr. some pool. Went home a while and then shot Ponce some pool in the late afternoon. He came by the room and talked of his trouble. His wife is hauling him into court Thursday for being behind $180 in child support. I gave him a $100 bill since his mother has agreed to help with the rest. Went to John T's for supper and joined George Gerault and some guy who teaches writing at Tulane. Walked down to the pool hall and shot pool with Ronnie who comes from Kansas City. Then we spent a while talking at the Royal Pub next to the hotel. Enjoyed him. Home to bed.

Smith once more! Although Sheppard didn't say it in so many words, I guessed he had again entered the man's apartment. From the description—"on my walk out Esplanade"—I formed an idea of the location of this residence.

> *Wednesday 4 January 1978*
> Saw John Smith in the morning and he went with me to pick up a Dutch 17th century landscape, which I bought from the Beasleys. Met Ponce at noon at Cigar's. He had won about $40 last night at pool and was planning to go to court $40 short and risk six months in prison. I gave him the $40 that he was short. Then went over to the Noble Arms to wait for the Whites' arrival. They got in at 3 P.M. and we walked down through the Quarter to the New Orleans Collection where they made a date for a tour in the A.M. at 10 before their boat trip on the Cotton Blossom. We then continued on down Royal Street to the tourism commission office where they got brochures on plantation trips and New Orleans. Then home for one hour rest, then over to John T's for dinner. Wonderful food. After supper they went to bed and I went to the pool hall where I played with a guy from N.Y. who is following the horses around the country. Then into bed late.

John Smith still again, with Sheppard probably starting the day at his apartment. Though I had no real choice in St. Petersburg, had I been in New Orleans, I would have needed to fight the urge to go looking for him without finishing my reading.

> *Thursday 5 January 1978*
> Up at break of dawn, breakfast in the Whites' room, then we walked up to Fauberg Marigny and looked at the old houses that are being restored. We walked back to the New Orleans Collection where they took a tour while I got them Johnny's Poor Boys and tickets for the Cotton Blossom. Came back and received the royal treatment from the director, etc.

Got out at one o'clock and went down to shoot pool. At 6 P.M. I picked up the car (Budget Rental) and back to Noble Arms where I picked up Ed and Ida for our dinner at LeRuth's in Gretna. A magnificent meal—one of the best the Whites ever had. I took them back after dinner and met Ponce at the pool hall. We played pool for a while, then went and talked, and Ponce broke down sobbing. The court experience had been agonizing for him and he was at the end of his reserves. "I want to wear a white shirt and tie when I go to work each day," he said. This touched me. He has never owned a suit of clothes. I gave him a note to Mr. Rubinstein so that he could purchase one on me at the Richmond Bros. sale.

*Friday 6 January 1978*

Met Ed and Ida at 7:30 A.M. and we drove to the Garden District. Parked at the corner of Jackson and Prytania and walked for two hours looking at the lovely Greek revival homes—we really liked this walk. Then out to see San Francisco, which is a garish and spectacular restoration, only a few months old but already falling prey to mildew and dampness. Then across the river to see Oak Alley. The exterior magnificent; the interior disappointingly furnished. Back to town. In the late afternoon see the Woodards and the McGhees who are joining us in town to see King Tut. Met Del and Truman on the street. We went to Richmond Bros. in time to see Ponce getting his suit. Del bought a handsome sport coat and we met at 7 P.M. at John T's where I gave the bunch a good dinner. Betty and Cathy and Del are planning to get up at 4 A.M. to get in line. I am taking the Whites around the Quarter and we will

> meet at Galatoere's for luncheon. Stopped and wished Ray Taylor a happy birthday, then over to the pool hall. We met at 6:30 P.M. at Del and Betty's room and went to Commander's Palace for dinner. The cost for 7 was $240 instead of $52 at John T's the night before. Food was equal. John Smith was to have come by but didn't. I met Larry Cephas and we shot pool and had a pleasant time. Later we went to the Golden Lantern where I shot pool with a hustler.

Ponce Woods and Larry Cephas owned alibis, so seeing their names didn't do much for me, but Smith definitely needed exploration as soon as possible.

> *Saturday 7 January 1978*
> In the early morning the Woodards and Whites walked up to the Beasley house and we looked it with a critical eye. The exterior woodwork is rotten and the roof is swaybacked. Decided that I'd reduce my offer at least $20,000 and ask for the furniture, too; in other words cross that house off the list. After our early walk, Ed and Ida met Truman and Cathy after mass planning to have brunch at Brennan's. Del, Betty, and I went back to John T's for our brunch after cancelling out the idea of going to Commander's jazz breakfast. When we were halfway through lunch, Truman and Cathy plus the Whites showed up. I went back to do a little last-minute packing before taking a cab to the Olivier Guest Home and picked up Del and Betty and left for the airport. (Candy called as I was leaving—24 hours late.)

Candy. The third acquaintance Sheppard's friends had mentioned during their interview with Heath and Melerine.

I would have to locate him, too, from that monster computer list of Candys in my desk at Homicide.

> *Sunday 8 January 1978*
> At the airport we had a drink and waited for our plane, which arrived a little late from L.A. Then to Tampa a little late. The limousine service is almost nonexistent and we hired a taxi who tried to crowd another two people into the car. It pissed me off mightily. We went to my house and had a nice omelet and a glass of wine. Went and saw A. late; he's decided to move in with Paula.

Mark Sheppard made no entries on the next five pages of his diary. Except for a pre-printed date in blue ink across the top and three small blue ink monthly calendars on the bottom, the twenty-four red ink lines were blank. He resumed his legible but compact and intense-looking script the following weekend:

> *Saturday 14 January 1978*
> Stopped early in the A.M. and saw Sam McClendon who seemed to be sullen. Went to the pool hall and started playing a charming kid, Mike. We played perhaps an hour and a half and I showed him some cars, then took him downtown to catch a bus home to Lake Wales to get his car. Enjoyed talking. Friendly feeling. I'll bet that I see him some more. At 4 P.M. I went to Moses Jones's wedding and sat with Paul Wallace. We didn't get done until 6:30 or 7 P.M. Went home and slept the clock around.
>
> Mike had promised to call, but didn't. We had talked of subject A and he wasn't upset.
>
> Memorable: Moses saying his vows to his wife,

Angela, with the tears running down his face. He really meant it! This made Mrs. Wallace misty-eyed, too.

*Sunday 15 January 1978*
Got up at 10:15 A.M. Called James and Rico, and I went to Pasadena Billiard. Both of them beat me so easily that I quit. Went by A for a while. Then cooked supper for Del and Betty. The praline parfait was superb. Did a stuffed eggplant with crab and shrimp, which can be rated only fair. The red beans and rice excellent. Sort of hoped that Mike might call today.

*Monday 16 January 1978*
Easy day in OR; done before noon. Saw Joe Bradham and signed will. Had him check around for mortgage money. Angelo came over in the afternoon; no Sherman Ray to work with. Had Chris come over for leftovers; then he went back to painting the guest house. Took Norman over to Tampa in the rabbit for a couple of drinks, then home to bed.

Tuesday, Wednesday, and Thursday's pages in the diary were jammed top to bottom, margin to margin, in a running missive, the last Mark Sheppard would ever write.

*Tuesday 17 January 1978*
Another short day; finished around noon. Got haircut. Shot pool at the Sportsman until 3 P.M., then over to see how Sherman was doing on the cars. Did some phoning and was taking a nap when Mike showed up. He had lost the phone number but

found the house. I was due to go with Del and Betty to dinner in 45 minutes. I had a whirlwind trip to see if we could rent Angelo's old apartment, but landlady not home; saw Chris so that in a pinch Mike could use the upstairs over the garage apartment on Beach Drive. Gave him money for supper and gas, then off to the Woodards. When we first started talking, Mike listed his problems mostly financial. He makes $168 a week and is buying a car, wants to buy his mother a car, and to repay $200 to his aunt who had loaned him money to go to school. He needs a place to stay in St. Pete and to pay $10 a week child support. He visualizes me as the answer to these problems. I can simply write a check and make all his problems disappear. As we talked I stressed self-help, independence, and his learning to cope with his problems. I said I would try to get him an apartment and pay the first month's rent to help him start solving his problems. We went down to see Winnie who wasn't home. Then I gave him a key to the house so that he could go to school that evening and then get back in and wait for me. Also gave him $20 for gas and something to eat. When I got home his car was in the driveway. Went upstairs where a light was burning. I found him sitting nude except for a dressing gown, which was lightly pulled closed around his middle. I went to the bed and propped myself up on pillows and we continued talking. He had just been sitting there, quietly waiting, looking into space, sipping a beer. Mike is well muscled, lean, 18 or 19 years old, about 6′1″ tall, maybe 180—no softening of fat under his dark skin, just muscle. He talked in a deep voice of his desire to get his mother a car. I suggested that Sherman (whom he'd met when we came in earlier) might be able to help him find something at the right price. I gave Sherman a call in Sarasota and put him on the lookout. I suggested that he call his aunt in Lake Wales. When he stood up to walk to the phone, his gown fell open and he showed an enormous erection, probably 10″ long (when dressed up, there was no clue of such equipment). He called his aunt and talked with an open dressing gown. Then he turned out the light and lay down on the bed and slipped out of the dressing gown. I sent him into the next room to sleep. About 20 minutes later he came back naked and again lay down beside me.

In the morning he almost wordlessly got dressed, turning his back while putting on his work clothes. He was to meet me at 9 A.M. and receive a call from his mother. When he was leaving he said, "Give me some money for breakfast." Took it and left. I didn't even hear the car go. Wednesday I was scheduled for a long day, but the first case ended in 15 minutes so I went down to see Winnie and made arrangements for his apartment. Gave Angelo some money, and went to the bank and drew cash for the trip to New Orleans and to pay for Mike's apartment. Then back to work. Went home, left Mike a letter of instructions on how to get the apartment and the money to do it with ($110), then back to work again. I rushed home at 10 P.M. No one there. Letter and money still on the chair. Went to bed. This morning when I was leaving for work I got a call. "Was tied up last night and couldn't get by. What about the apartment?" I told him that I had made arrangements yesterday, but that was yesterday and the deal was off this morning, and I had to leave for work. He wanted to

> get some money to go to Lakeland tonight. I said "sorry," but that I'd be back Sunday. Warned him not to come in while I was away on account of the burglar alarm and hung up. Quick case. Brought Angelo home. Nancy and Angelo did my packing, and I had the locksmith fit a new lock and keys to the back door. Left Nancy and Angelo joking and having fun as I drove to the airport with the bust of Andrew Jackson packed in a suitcase for the New Orleans Historical Collection. Tonight I take Larry Cephas to dinner at John T's. Chris came by—the upstairs apartment is about to be rented. I told him not to let Mike use it as previously planned until Sunday.

And so ended the soap-opera saga of the wealthy, middle-aged anesthesiologist whose newly opened chapter on Mike would remain forever unfinished. The doctor didn't see him on Sunday or ever again.

But John Smith deserved urgent attention. It was his home Sheppard had entered, doing what I'd been assured the doctor would never dare.

It was 5:00 A.M. in Florida, an hour earlier in New Orleans. Fred would be on graveyard.

"Monk," I said, using Dantagnan's nickname (some in Homicide thought he resembled a fierce, mad monk). "It's John. What's going on?"

"What's going on? It's four in the morning. The rest of the world will be waking up soon and I'll be going to bed. Are you feeling okay?"

"Fine. I might have something on the Sheppard case."

"How's your stomach?"

"Fine. Can you get into the computer? Is it up?"

"The doctor tells you to take a month off with no stress, and you're in Florida worrying about the computer, before daylight no less. Smart move, Dillmann. At this rate, Diane will collect your pension, and I'll have to stand in as father of the bride at Amy's wedding."

"Give me a break, Fred. How's Bea and the kids?"

"At least they see me once in a while. When are you coming back?"

"Later today, I think. Look, Fred, I need a favor."

"What favor? Help put you back in the hospital? Jesus Christ, John, you're a grown man. Why don't you use your head?"

"This is important. Listen, Fred, I . . ."

"What do you want?"

"Run this name in the computer: John Smith."

"Are you sober? Do you know how many John Smiths will pour out of that machine?"

"Yeah. His mom really racked her brain to name him."

"Can't you give me a little help? Like race. Age. Anything?"

"Only that he lives around Esplanade and Marais. Pull a list of any John Smiths in that vicinity."

"Who is this guy?"

"A friend of Sheppard's. As far as I can tell, the *only one* he ever visited alone in a New Orleans residence. It's a real longshot, but give it a whirl."

"Okay. I'll get back to you in an hour."

Always as good as his word, the phone rang forty-five minutes later.

"John?"

"Yeah. Fred."

"I may have something. John E. Smith. Black male, born August 3, 1956. Last known address: 1451 St. Claude Avenue, just a few blocks from Esplanade."

"What does his rap look like?"

"He's a Quarter rat. Been stopped several times. Three felonies and a misdemeanor. Three of the busts were for possession of a controlled substance, the other for criminal trespass."

"Anything else?"

"I always save the best for last."

"What is it?"

"Mr. Smith goes by the alias Candy."

# • 10 •

No John Smith at the St. Claude address. Ditto for Cigar's. People there said it had been a long time since they had seen him.

On February 26, armed with a picture of John E. "Candy" Smith, I canvassed the neighborhood of Marais and Esplanade, knocking on doors of houses and lower-income apartment buildings. No one I talked with admitted knowing the young black man with model's looks and a weightlifter's strong, lithe physique, a muscle type who hustled pool and, I suspected, anything else, including his body.

I believed any arrest might be difficult and dangerous, and if I did succeed in locating him, I intended to bring along hefty backup. To throttle an individual the way Mark Sheppard had been murdered required considerable strength, exactly what leaped out at me from mug shots of the powerful John Edward Smith.

I passed out pictures to every police officer who worked the neighborhood, asked them to tune their ears carefully for any street talk, and check again with their informants. I visited narcotics district officers, requesting each one also to tap their sources. I spoke with the detectives who had busted Candy on those drug raps (they didn't know where he might be), and with employees of the bonding companies that had bailed him out of jail.

I kept leaning hard on the pool hustlers and other characters that hung out at Cigar's. John Smith had been a regular there—someone had to know about him and his whereabouts.

Bill "Cigar" Barr (he actually used Cigar as his middle name) told me the publicity had been good for business. He had been interviewed by *Times-Picayune* reporters, and by several newspapers in Florida. As word of Sheppard's sexual preference spread in St. Petersburg, the retirement community found little else to talk about. The case became a cause célèbre in St. Pete, generating much more interest there than in New Orleans.

Finally I got a lead: A beat cop told me Smith had a girlfriend, Daisy Scott, who lived at the 1451 St. Claude Avenue address. Clearly, Candy had used Daisy's address when he got busted.

I soon discovered a double switch: A check of welfare rolls revealed that several payments had been mailed to Daisy at 1423 Marais Street, smack in the area Dr. Sheppard had written about. Though far too early to draw conclusions, I remembered the woman's pantyhose wrapped around the doctor's neck.

On March 3, 1978, accompanied by Homicide Detectives Richard Baumy and Robert Egan, I went to Marais Street to find John Smith.

The narrow but deep two-story wood frame building at 1423 Marais—a lovely home back in the nineteenth century—had been converted to ten apartments and now qualified, in my mind, as a slum dwelling. Similar structures stood on each side of 1423, and narrow alleyways ran from the street to apartments in the rear.

I knocked on a first-floor door fronting the street, and showed my badge to the young black woman who answered. "We're looking for a guy named Candy who lives in one of these apartments," I said. "Can you tell me which one?"

"I don't know any Candy."

"What's your name?"

"Catherine."

"Catherine what?" I hated teeth-pulling-type questioning. Many people either don't want to cooperate with police, or don't want to *appear* to be cooperating.

"Catherine Crutchfield."

"Catherine, how long have you lived here?"

"About a year."

"Look at this picture, please." I held up one of John Smith's mug shots. "Look at it closely. Have you ever seen this man?"

"I've seen him."

"Where?"

"In the back," she answered, motioning toward the alleyway.

"Do you know which apartment?"

"No. I've only seen him coming and going through the alley."

In single file, Baumy and Egan followed me to the rear of 1423 Marais, stepping over discarded beer cans and broken bottles. It was a warm, perfect March morning, spring in New Orleans, and I felt my heart beat a little faster.

We walked up three steps at the rear of the building into a dirty, sunless, enclosed hallway, and I pounded the door on the left which had been marked "B" in crayon.

Again a young black woman answered and I showed my ID.

"What's your name?" I asked.

"Beverly."

I looked at Egan.

"Beverly what?"

"Beverly Smith."

"Are you any relation to John Smith?"

"I don't know any John Smith."

"How about Candy? Do you know a dude named Candy?"

"No."

"Please look at this picture. Have you ever seen this man?"

Recognition flickered across her face. She stared for a few moments, then, without a word, pointed her right index finger to the ceiling. John Smith lived upstairs.

"Which apartment?" I asked.

"Apartment D. Right above me," she said softly.

"Does he live alone?"

"No. He lives with some young dude. And there's a chick they call Daisy who comes around a lot. Look, officer, is there gonna be trouble? Should I leave?"

"No. Just stay inside."

My heart picked up more speed as we climbed the unlit, curved stairwell to apartment D. We pressed ourselves against the wall on either side of the door and drew our guns. I cocked the .357 Smith and Wesson with the four-inch nickel-plated barrel, and knocked.

"Who is it?"

"Police!"

*"What?"*

"Police!"

The door opened—slowly. A white guy in his mid-twenties, and a white woman standing beside him, their eyes big as saucers, stared at us, three men in suits with guns drawn. We quickly put the weapons away—whoever these two were, they weren't John Smith and Daisy Scott—and identified ourselves as police officers.

"I'm Curtis McKnight," the apartment resident said. "This is my wife Karen."

"May we come inside. We need to talk to you."

"Yeah, come in. What's the problem?"

"No problem. Just a few questions. How long have you and your wife lived here?"

"About three weeks. Since February 9." He glanced around the apartment: small living room, tiny kitchen, bedroom, bathroom. All visible from where we stood. "We're looking for a better place."

"Are you working?"

"I'm a waiter at Antoine's."

One of the three best restaurants in the city. Great French and Creole food. I figured McKnight would soon be able to afford better housing.

"Do you know who rented this apartment before you?"

"I have no idea."

Taking the mug shot out of my pocket, I asked, "Have you ever seen this man around the building?"

McKnight and his wife looked and shook their heads.

We were standing in the living room, and while they studied the photo, I took a closer look around. My eyes stopped on a cluster of droplets on the wall near the front door. I edged closer, and didn't have a doubt in the world. I had seen blood so often I believed I could recognize it anywhere.

"Curtis," I said, over my shoulder, "what's this?" I indicated the reddish brown stains.

"Beats me. It was there when we moved in."

But I knew. And so did Baumy and Egan.

"Curtis," I said, "we think someone might have been hurt in this apartment before you occupied it. Do you mind if we look around a little more?"

"Go ahead."

"Are you renting this apartment furnished or unfurnished?"

"Unfurnished. Except for a bed and dresser that were here when we came."

Detectives dig up many more losers than winners. Like hardnosed old prospectors panning for gold, we survive on bits and pieces from small veins of ore that peter out quickly. Rarely do we strike it rich. The three of us searched the apartment, and it was one of those rare times.

At apartment D on 1423 Marais Street we hit the mother lode, an evidentiary gold mine.

The blood droplets near the front door were just a hint, a teaser, of what would follow. The shabby apartment had many terrible secrets to reveal, and so clear were they to a trained eye that, had the dwelling been human, I believed it would just have been waiting for our overdue arrival to blurt out the savage scene it had witnessed.

Several times, as my gaze traveled from living room to kitchen to bathroom to bedroom and out to the dingy enclosed hallway, I wanted to punch my fist into the air and shout "Eureka!"

A detective can devote a lifetime to the job and never encounter a case such as Sheppard's, and ten lifetimes before finding *this* murder scene. It was so much sweeter, this dream moment for a cop, because a good, professional investigation led us to the find.

Not that I considered any of these things as I moved from spot to spot, lost in a private world. I don't remember saying anything to Baumy, Egan, or the McKnights. Only seeing, imagining, hoping.

The crime-scene search began when I walked into the bedroom and noticed a two-inch blood smear on the door frame leading to the bathroom. In the bathroom itself, I saw signs of violence—large amounts of dried, caked blood—on the floor right up against the baseboards.

I crouched down on my hands and knees and looked closer. The floor, I was sure, had once been a river of blood. Apparently someone had done a hurried, sloppy mop-up, swabbing the blood into cracks between the baseboard and the flooring. Using my pocketknife, I scraped a portion of dried residue out of a crack and smeared the blade across my hand. No doubt about it. Blood, and it hadn't come from a shaving nick or a nosebleed. There was too much of it. The words of the coroner whispered in my head: "Trauma to right temple."

Back to the bedroom: The double bed Curtis McKnight said had come with the apartment appeared to be the perfect size for that yellow fitted bedsheet found wrapped around Mark Sheppard's head.

I went to the living room and conducted a hands-and-knees search of the floor. Bingo! Three more drops of blood formed a delicate trail from the bathroom to the front door.

It was so dark in the hallway Baumy had to fetch a flashlight from the car.

Board by board under the shining flashlight, excitement growing, I searched the hallway and down the stairs to the door leading outside. *On the entire trip,* on every stair but two, I found at least one drop of blood!

I discovered the clincher on the curvature of the stairwell: a bloody handprint. It was approximately four feet up the wall, an appropriate level for someone bearing a heavy load to grasp for support.

The blood trail led me all the way to the alley. I continued to the car and radioed for a crime lab team.

Leaning against the vehicle, I pictured Dr. Sheppard's lifeless body being carried from a pool of blood on the bathroom floor, through the living room, down the stairwell, and outside to a waiting car. From there it had been driven to Almonaster and dumped into the swamp. The bloody handprint testified to the difficulty the perpetrators had negotiating the curvature of the stairs.

No doubt, I thought, it took two to carry the body. Surely John Smith, Candy, had been one of them. Had the other been Daisy Scott? Or, more likely, the unknown roommate?

Crime lab technician Keith Valteau and criminalist Charles Krone arrived on the scene. Under my direction they took two dozen photos—mostly of the smears, droplets, and splatters—and carefully collected samples from various locations along the blood trail. Valteau attempted to lift fingerprints from the handprint on the stairwell, but failed because of what he called an "unsuitable surface." Glass is the easiest surface to print; wood, because of the grain, the most difficult.

Documenting, dusting, collecting, measuring, Valteau and Krone stayed with me for three hours, getting everything just right. (Baumy and Egan returned to their own cases.) The crime scene, considered critical, is almost always *the* most important source for the evidence prosecutors love: the physical variety, of which we found plenty.

Sheppard's diary clearly indicated that the only private New Orleans residence he had visited alone was John Smith's apartment, which now showed *physical evidence* that a violent crime had been committed there. We knew Sheppard's body had been dumped, and the blood trail leading out of the apartment, blood on the steps, and the handprint were highly suggestive of a body being carried down the stairs.

John Smith had become a prime suspect. This had been

*his* apartment. Sheppard had visited it. Even the most dull-witted detective would consider Candy the likely killer.

I had to bring myself down to earth. Clearly, celebrations had to be avoided until we located the third crucial element of any murder trilogy. We had two key ingredients: the body and the scene of the crime.

I gave Price periodic updates on how the investigation fared. When I told him about the findings on Marais, he agreed that "When you find John Smith, you solve the case."

The most avid and supportive followers of the investigation were my fellow homicide detectives. Virtually every one of them had put in significant time on the case, and I felt their eyes looking over my shoulder. Good. It provided incentive for peak performance.

Even Diane forgot I was supposed to be resting and gearing down my pace when I brought her news of the discoveries at Candy's former apartment. She asked if I thought John Smith was involved (yes), whether I believed him extremely dangerous (yes, but I told her no), and did I intend to question him personally (I certainly hoped so).

But first we had to find him. Also, I wanted to collect as much information as possible—not the least the crime lab report—before our face-to-face confrontation.

The Marais Street news took the heat off Duffy by mellowing Morris. We had a hot suspect and it was only a matter of time before we brought him in. The twice-a-day phone calls from Chief Morris demanding results suddenly stopped. Indeed, had I run into him, I guessed he would have a few words of praise, something like, "You've done a fine job, Dantagnan." He always called me "Dantagnan," and he addressed Fred as "Dillmann."

While waiting for the crime lab report, I called on Roland

Gee, landlord of the Marais residence, who lived in the comfortable suburb of Metairie. Gee told me he rented the apartment on November 4, 1977, to John Smith, whom he positively identified from the mug shot. Gee said Candy lived at the apartment with an unknown male, had been visited frequently by a young woman named Daisy, and had moved out on January 30, 1978. The landlord described the roommate as black, about eighteen years old, light-skinned, very slender, and more than six feet tall.

Of course, I looked for Candy. Several times I pulled long stakeouts at 1451 St. Claude, Daisy Scott's address, but never caught a glimpse of him. I also kept an eye on Cigar's, reemphasizing to Barr that he needed to contact me the moment he spotted Candy. Every uniform in the French Quarter now had his picture and instructions to detain him as a murder suspect.

The crime lab delivered its report on March 7:

Evidence Received: 3-3-78
Type of Investigation: MURDER
Examination Requested: BLOOD, HAIR
Subject: JOHN SMITH
Victim: DR. MARK SHEPPARD
Specimens:

1) BLOOD SAMPLES REMOVED FROM BATHROOM, LIVING ROOM, AND STAIRWELL OF APARTMENT AT 1423 MARAIS STREET.
2) ONE YELLOW BOTTOM BED SHEET REMOVED FROM DR. SHEPPARD'S BODY.

Results:

1) SPECIMEN ONE YIELDED POSITIVE SEROLOGICAL TESTS FOR GROUP B HUMAN BLOOD.
2) SPECIMEN TWO YIELDED POSITIVE SEROLOGICAL TESTS FOR HUMAN BLOOD; HOWEVER, ATTEMPTS TO GROUP THE BLOOD WERE UNSUCCESSFUL.

3) HAIRS REMOVED FROM SPECIMEN TWO WERE CHARACTERISTIC FOR THE NEGROID AND CAUCASIAN RACE.

—CHARLES KRONE
CRIMINALIST

A mixed bag, I decided. The good news: I needed only to learn Sheppard's blood type to match it with that found in the apartment and stairwell. The bad: The amount of blood on the fitted yellow bedsheet hadn't been sufficient to type.

I called Price in St. Petersburg and asked him to find out Sheppard's blood type.

"No problem," he said.

# • 11 •

I'VE logged it the strangest conversation I ever had.

"Are you Daisy Scott?" it began. I had simply become frustrated with the fruitless stakeouts of 1451 St. Claude, and decided to make a direct approach. Detective John McKenzie stood beside me, and Detective Louis Munsch had gone around to cover the rear.

"I'm Daisy." She wore a bright flowered housecoat and I put her age at twenty-five.

"Police officers." I held up my badge and tried a bluff. "Tell Candy to come outside. I want to talk to him."

"Candy's not here." The words coming from Daisy Scott's mouth were clear enough, but her body language told a different story. In a loud voice she said, "I haven't seen him for a week."

But her contorting facial muscles and air-fanning hands gestured, *follow me.* She backed inside.

McKenzie and I eased over the threshold. "He lives here, doesn't he?" I boomed, trying to match her volume.

She continued walking backward, hands indicating *come on,* her face full of fear. "No," she said in a husky voice. "He comes by sometimes, but he doesn't stay."

"Where is his place?" I asked, not quite so loudly. I signalled Daisy, *decrease the volume,* to make it sound like we still stood on the porch.

Without missing a beat, she continued the overplayed conversation we now used to muffle giveaway creaks from the floorboards. "Look, officer, I don't want no trouble. It's just me and my little boy here, and we don't need no problems."

We had advanced fifteen feet inside the residence. Daisy kept backing up, gesturing, guiding the tiptoe advance of me and McKenzie.

"I'll only ask one more time. Where is his place?"

"On Touro Street." She went another step backward. Two.

"Where on Touro Street?" I had the Smith and Wesson out.

"I don't know," she said, backing toward the bathroom on her left. "But I'll go with you. Maybe I can show you the house."

She'd been backing up bent slightly forward at the waist, but now straightened up triumphantly, a fierce smile on her face, and pointed to a cupboard underneath the sink. Munsch had unholstered his weapon and had it aimed at the cupboard's door.

I reached down gingerly with my left hand, holding the .38 in my right, and whipped open the door. "Come out of there, scumbag!" I ordered. "Hands out first!"

Nothing. We had our guns aimed right at the cupboard's opening.

"Come out!"

Two hands slowly, tentatively, crept out of the aperture, followed by arms, and the moment I saw his head my gun was pressed against it. McKenzie seized Smith's wrists and pulled him out onto the floor. I placed my foot on the back of his neck, McKenzie handcuffed him, and together we yanked Candy to his feet. I immediately advised him of his rights, that he was a suspect in a murder investigation.

"I didn't do anything," he said. "Don't hurt me. I didn't do anything."

I took Daisy aside, thanked her, and we led the muscular Smith out to my car. When I was behind the wheel, I again read him his rights.

"What's this all about?" he asked, fear in his eyes.

"I'll talk to you later," I said.

"I haven't done anything."

I called the dispatcher, gave him a "Ten Fifteen": prisoner coming. Before knocking on the door to Daisy Scott's apartment, I had radioed a "Ten Ninety-seven": arrived at scene. The dispatcher logged the time of each message, effectively short-cutting any future defense attorney claim that I drove Smith around for several hours, beat him, and thus made possible a confession. Looking back, I know I did everything by the book, dotted every "i," crossed every "t."

Everybody in Homicide was up and looking when I brought Candy in. I placed him in an interrogation room, and stepped outside to talk with Duffy.

"You got him!" Duffy enthused. "Fine work."

"I hope so. But this'll be our only chance."

We needed a confession. We had no witnesses, so despite the blood in his former apartment, and the fact that search warrants might uncover the source of the electrical cord, a good lawyer could make it tough without a confession. It was almost a rule of thumb that a detective got one opportunity to obtain a confession, and then the suspect asked for an attorney.

"Take your best shot, John," Duffy said.

* * *

I walked back into the interrogation room, took off the handcuffs, sat down opposite Smith, and stared at him. Sweat poured off his body, like a horse lathered just before a big race. After a few minutes I read him his rights a *third* time.

"John," I said, "do you understand what I've told you three times? That you're a suspect in a murder investigation?"

He nodded affirmatively.

I kept staring at him. "You know you're here because of Doctor Sheppard, don't you?"

He put his head on his chest. His eyes, filled with hopelessness, gazed at the floor.

"I know Doctor Sheppard died in your apartment," I said. "You have a choice: Tell me freely and voluntarily what happened, or keep your mouth shut and we'll do it the hard way. It's up to you."

He raised his eyes, and I thought I saw a glimmer of hope. "I didn't kill him," he said. "I swear to you. I didn't kill him. They were supposed to just rob him."

I needed to tape-record Smith, and I asked Sergeant Steve London into the 12×8 interrogation room, a cubicle sparsely furnished with a solid metal table and three brown folding chairs. The room, clean, gray, antiseptic, had only one unusual feature, a two-way mirror in the wall behind which someone—usually a superior—could watch and listen to the statement being taken. I suspected Tom Duffy would be there this March 9, just before noon, hoping to witness the breakthrough for which we had worked so hard.

Normally I would have conducted the interview alone, but I had been pushing myself for several weeks and couldn't risk blowing the case at this critical juncture. If we succeeded in taping the confession, it would be the centerpiece of any trial, and the defense attorney would bore holes into it, move heaven and earth, to see it discredited.

London and I sat at one side of the table, Smith on the other. The moment of truth had arrived. Our suspect looked at us benignly, almost as if we were friends, his demeanor having undergone a sea change. He now seemed relaxed, composed, extremely confident. As I snapped on the tape recorder, I couldn't imagine why.

LONDON: John, would you please identify yourself?

SMITH: John Edward Smith. I'm twenty-one years of age.

LONDON: Where do you live, John?

SMITH: Right now, I'm living at Toulouse, 2900 block of Toulouse.

LONDON: John, I want to again formally advise you that you are under arrest for the murder of Doctor Mark Sheppard. I will now, again, advise you of your rights. You need not make any statements, that is, you have a right to remain silent. Anything you say may be used against you in trial. You have the right to consult with and obtain the advice of an attorney before answering any questions. If you cannot afford an attorney, the court will obtain an attorney to represent you and advise you. You have a right to have your attorney or an appointed attorney present at the time of any questioning or the giving of any statement. Do you understand what I have just told you?

SMITH: I do.

LONDON: Is it your desire to waive these rights and make this statement?

SMITH: It is.

This marked the *fourth* time Smith had been advised of his rights. We aimed to take a statement that could withstand the strongest assault.

LONDON: Has anybody threatened or beaten you into giving this taped statement?
SMITH: They haven't.

London and I knew he would change his tune in court. It was standard operating procedure for a defendant to claim his confession had been brutalized out of him. I owned two one hundred percent perfect records in this regard: I *never* beat a suspect, and I *always* got accused of it.

LONDON: Have you been promised anything in return for this statement?
SMITH: No, I have not.
LONDON: Are you handcuffed at this time?
SMITH: No, I am not.
LONDON: How many police officers are present in the room at the time of this statement?
SMITH: One.

Jesus. London and I sat right in front of him, and he answered "one."

LONDON: No, there are . . .
SMITH: Two.
LONDON: Do you know their names?
SMITH: No, I don't.
LONDON: Let this tape reflect that Detective John Dillmann and Sergeant Steve London are present. John, let me direct your attention to Friday,

January 20, 1978, at approximately 9:00 A.M. Can you tell me what occurred at this time?

SMITH: On Friday?

LONDON: On Friday.

SMITH: On Friday morning at nine there were two dudes waiting to rip off the doc. I didn't even want them to rip the doc off, but they insisted, they needed the money, so I gave them the permission to go ahead, they could rip him off. But I never knew that anything like this was going to take place until it happened, and after it had happened, it was too late for me to really do something. Well, maybe I should have did something, I could have did something, but I was just silent and just let it go ahead. I hadn't did no crime, well, I didn't think I had committed no crime, I hadn't murdered nobody. I mean, I was a witness, I was there, I seen . . .

I had halfway expected him to say he hadn't killed Sheppard, and didn't for a moment believe him. What we chose to accept, however, counted for nothing. The story he proceeded to relate made him just as guilty as those he implicated, but Smith didn't know this. He had no conception of felony murder laws, no conception of anything, really. He sat relaxed, talked calmly, supremely confident the story he told would absolve him. The average citizen needs to hear a statement like this to believe it, yet it is the norm, not the exception. Homicide cops seldom if ever deal with a Professor Moriarty. This statement I believed as commonplace as the name of the man who gave it, could have been used in a training manual for detectives, illustrating perfectly what they would likely encounter.

LONDON: John, how long have you known Doctor Sheppard?

SMITH: Since 1976, 1977.

LONDON: Could you describe your relationship with Doctor Sheppard?

SMITH: Well, yeah, the doc took a great interest in me. He said I had a nice body, and he just took a like to me.

LONDON: Have you seen him often?

SMITH: Yes, I see him every time he come into town. He would have a way for me to know his telephone number so I could call him and let me know where he was at, and leave me a key.

LONDON: This address, 1423 Marais, apartment D, is that where you used to reside?

SMITH: Yes.

LONDON: Would you please explain to us how Doctor Sheppard came to be at 1423 Marais Street, apartment D, on Friday, January 20, 1978?

SMITH: All right. On Thursday afternoon, all of us were in the pool hall shooting pool and I sat with the doc for a while and he said he had some kind of dinner. He had to go to dinner with someone, so he said he would see me that morning, that Friday morning 'cause we already had decided that from Thursday afternoon, that he was going to come to see me that Friday morning. So, that's how he eventually came there 'cause he had already decided that he was going to come over there.

This had the absolute ring of truth. Billy Barr had said Candy had been in Cigar's that Thursday afternoon, that only later had he barred him from the establishment. Soon we learned John Smith had been extremely jealous of Ponce Woods receiving that pool cue.

LONDON: Would you please relate everything from the moment he entered your apartment, everything that transpired and occurred that Friday morning.

SMITH: Doc came in. I was in the bedroom. As you know, this is a three-room apartment, bedroom, living room, and kitchen, and I was in the bedroom. The doc came in, he said, "Good morning." He took off his clothes and went to the bathroom. Okay, that's the only thing that occurred. He go to the bathroom, and they put a gun to his head and told him to lay to the floor which he did, and . . .

LONDON: Who did this?

SMITH: Patin. So, they searched him for money. He didn't have no money on him, but I think forty dollars. That's about all that took place. They decided that the doc could identify them if they were to just took the forty dollars and left, so they wanted to know what to do, what to do, what to do. So, they came up with the idea to kill him, you know, so they did.

LONDON: All right, how did they? Describe to me exactly what occurred inside the bathroom.

SMITH: He took a cord off a radio that I have and put it around his neck and took a sock and stuck it in his mouth to keep him from screaming.

Only someone present could have known about the cord around the neck and the sock stuck in the mouth. These were pieces of information withheld from the press, and

Smith's admissions couldn't have been more damaging to his cause.

LONDON: Did the doctor struggle at any time while this happened?

SMITH: No, he wanted to say something, but the dude wouldn't let him speak, you know. I don't know what it was, but he tried to say something, but he wouldn't let him say nothing. So, he didn't put up no struggle.

LONDON: What was your participation in this?

SMITH: Well, at first, I was frightened, you know, I was very scared. I had never seen nothing like this take place, and I wanted to run, but if I had run, you know, it still would took place in my, you know, all this took place where I live. And if I had ran, either way, it would still be on me, you know. So, after it had happened, I just told them like it was. I said, well, you all going to have to dispose of him from here because this is where I live, and I did stay there until at least about two or three weeks after.

LONDON: John, how did they remove the body of Doctor Sheppard from your apartment?

SMITH: By carrying him downstairs.

LONDON: All right, did they wrap him in anything?

SMITH: They had a sheet off my bed.

Absolutely true. This statement alone, I believed, dug Smith's grave.

LONDON: Would you describe that sheet?

SMITH: Yellow sheet. And a bag, a garbage bag, a trash

bag, they pulled that over him, and they took him out to the car.

Smith couldn't have been more right. Or more guilty. As I re-read the transcribed confession, I feel something akin to despair.

LONDON: Did they take him out to the car in the daytime, or was it in the night?
SMITH: It was in the night.
DILLMANN: During the course of your involvement with Doctor Sheppard, did you become involved in any sexual relations?
SMITH: Yes.
DILLMANN: Was this one time, twice, numerous occasions?
SMITH: I had sex with him more than a dozen times.
DILLMANN: Would he give you money, presents, or anything?
SMITH: He would give me money and buy me whatever I wanted.
DILLMANN: John, do you have a nickname?
SMITH: People call me Candy.
DILLMANN: Are you from here originally?
SMITH: I was born in the city, but I was raised in Pensacola, Florida.
DILLMANN: During the course of your relationship with Doctor Sheppard, did you ever have occasion to visit him in Florida?
SMITH: Yes. He sent me a ticket and I came and lived with him there about a week.
DILLMANN: Do you remember when that was, John?
SMITH: Not exactly, I don't remember, you know, the exact time, the date or whatever it was, but I do remember that I stayed with him for about a week.

DILLMANN: That was in his home in St. Petersburg, correct?

SMITH: Yes, right.

DILLMANN: And you say you stayed with him for about a week at that time?

SMITH: Yes.

DILLMANN: Did you meet any of his friends there?

SMITH: I did.

DILLMANN: So, these people in St. Pete would know you from this visit?

SMITH: Right.

DILLMANN: Who did you reside with at the Marais Street address? Who lived there with you, John?

SMITH: Oh, I lived with a partner of mine. His name is Red. That's the only name I know him by, is Red. That's all we ever called him.

DILLMANN: Did he move in with you when you first rented the place?

SMITH: No, he didn't. I had been staying there and he told me one day that his mom was going to put him out and he needed a place to stay, but he had a job, so quite naturally, I let him stay.

DILLMANN: Do you know anything else about Red? Do you know his mother, his father, his sisters, brothers?

SMITH: Never met none of his relatives.

DILLMANN: Do you know where he worked?

SMITH: He used to work off of Decatur. He don't work there no more. He quit that job.

DILLMANN: To your knowledge, he's just a hustler from in the Quarter? Is that correct?

SMITH: That's right.

DILLMANN: Can you give me a description of Red?

SMITH: Oh, about six-one or six-two.

DILLMANN: He's a black male, right?
SMITH: He's a black male.
DILLMANN: About how old would you say he is?
SMITH: Seventeen or eighteen, something like that.
DILLMANN: How much would you say he weighs?
SMITH: About one twenty-five, one thirty, somewhere like that.
DILLMANN: Does he have any hair on his face? A moustache, goatee, anything?
SMITH: No, nothing.
DILLMANN: How about his hair? Does he have a large Afro, or is it close cropped?
SMITH: It's a little bush.
DILLMANN: Do you know anything else at all about Red?
SMITH: I don't.
DILLMANN: Do you know where Red could be located?
SMITH: I'm not sure.
DILLMANN: How long have you known Red, John?
SMITH: About five months.
DILLMANN: And during this whole five-month period, he has never told you his last name?
SMITH: No.
DILLMANN: You've never asked him his last name?
SMITH: No.
DILLMANN: Do you know any of his friends?
SMITH: Harold Patin, that's the only one.
DILLMANN: Who actually strangled the doctor?
SMITH: Patin and Red.
DILLMANN: Both?
SMITH: Yes.
DILLMANN: You also mention that a sock was placed in Doctor Sheppard's mouth. Is that correct?
SMITH: Yes. They were looking for something to put in his mouth and they seen the sock and they

Ursulines Guest House. (*Don Guillot*)

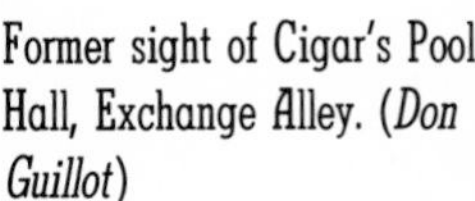

Former sight of Cigar's Pool Hall, Exchange Alley. (*Don Guillot*)

Dick Price. (*Darrell Farley*)

Entrance to Dr. Sheppard's home, St. Petersburg, Florida. (*Dick Price*)

Dr. Mark Sheppard. (*New Orleans Police Department*)

Candy. Photo found in Dr. Sheppard's home. (*New Orleans Police Department*)

Dr. Sheppard's clothing, found near his body. (*New Orleans Police Department*)

Alley leading to entrance of upstairs apartment where Dr. Sheppard was killed. (*New Orleans Police Department*)

Stairs leading to murder scene. Note blood droplets on floor. (*New Orleans Police Department*)

Murder scene. Note blood on floor and baseboards. (*New Orleans Police Department*)

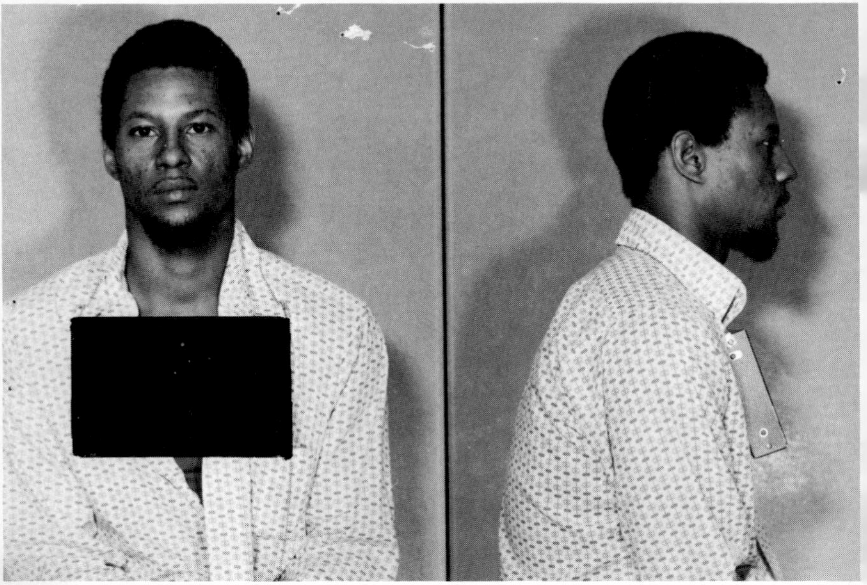

Harold Patin. (*New Orleans Police Department*)

Joe Meyer, Assistant District Attorney. (*Don Guillot*)

Buddy Lemann, Defense Attorney. (*Don Guillo*

just decided to put it in his mouth. That's what they did.

DILLMANN: How many times would you say that Doctor Sheppard had been to your apartment?

SMITH: This was the second time.

DILLMANN: It was only the second time? When was the first?

SMITH: Just before this visit. He had made one visit, only about two or three weeks beforehand.

Smith had the whole story. This first visit had been documented in Sheppard's diary.

DILLMANN: Getting back to Thursday, January 19, 1978, you mentioned that you were shooting pool in Cigar's. Was that when you made arrangements with Doctor Sheppard to come to your apartment the next day?

SMITH: Something like that. He was going to take someone out to dinner, and he wanted to know if it was all right that we could get together that morning. So, I said, yeah. Well, he asked me do I still live there. I said, yeah. He said, why don't I drop by in the morning.

DILLMANN: Was Harold Patin or Red in the pool hall at that time?

SMITH: Harold was in there with me.

DILLMANN: Am I correct that Doctor Sheppard was coming to your apartment on the morning of January 20, 1978, to engage in sexual relations with you? Is that correct?

SMITH: Right.

DILLMANN: Now, after he left the pool hall, who approached you, or were you approached? How did your conversation originate about ripping off the doctor? Would you relate that to me in detail?

SMITH: I passed back by the pool hall about ten and there was nobody in there, so I left. Then I ran into the other little dude, Red, and we talked, and he was telling me about how bad hustling was, and people weren't buying nothing, and he needed some money, and this and that. And they decided that if I knew the doc and he just came in town that he would be a good person for them to rip off.

He was making clear that they intended to commit a felony, which meant he could be charged with first-degree murder.

DILLMANN: John, now when you say rip off, do you mean they were going to rob the doctor?

SMITH: Right.

DILLMANN: They were going to rob him of his money?

SMITH: That's all they said.

DILLMANN: And you knew that the next morning they were going to rob him of his money?

SMITH: Right, I did.

DILLMANN: And they were going to use your apartment as the place to rob him of his money? Is that correct?

SMITH: Right.

While Smith self-confidently thought he was passing off on someone else a murder I firmly believed *he* had committed, in reality he was convicting himself. I suspected that Duffy, watching from behind that two-way glass, already anticipated the pleasure of relaying the good news to Chief Morris.

DILLMANN: The express purpose of their being at your apartment was to perpetrate an armed robbery on Doctor Mark Sheppard, is that correct?
SMITH: Yes.
DILLMANN: And you had knowledge of this?
SMITH: Yes. I did. Well, I didn't have no knowledge of this armed robbery. All I know was that they were going to take the money. I didn't know, you know, that there was going to be no armed robbery.
DILLMANN: But you knew they were going to rob him?
SMITH: Right.

Once again his own words convicted him of first-degree murder. He thought himself shrewd and cunning, but the opposite was true.

DILLMANN: All right, were you going to get any of the money from the robbery?
SMITH: All I was doing was letting them be in my apartment. At that time I had money, so I didn't need no money. I was just letting them make them some money.

John E. "Candy" Smith the humanitarian. Would anybody believe this?

DILLMANN: You weren't going to get any of the money?
SMITH: No. If I wanted any money, I was going to get it anyway, you know, 'cause all I had to do was ask for it.

DILLMANN: You were just furnishing them a place to rob Doctor Sheppard, that's what it amounted to?

SMITH: Yes, that's what it amounted to.

DILLMANN: How did Red and Harold find out that the doctor was going to be at your apartment Friday morning?

SMITH: I told them.

DILLMANN: Why did you tell them?

SMITH: I just told them so that they could make some money.

LONDON: Didn't you think that if they robbed Doctor Sheppard in your apartment with you there, and then left and didn't do anything to Doctor Sheppard, that Doctor Sheppard would naturally know who you are and could go to the police and say you assisted in this robbery? Didn't you think about that?

SMITH: Well, I had figured that the doc was going to recognize them. Well, I thought that he would.

LONDON: All right, you thought he would, so you previously stated in this tape that the reason Doctor Sheppard was killed is because he could make an identification. Is that correct?

SMITH: Uh-huh.

LONDON: Well, then you must have known that he was going to be killed ahead of time.

SMITH: I didn't know that they was going to kill him, no. All I thought, they were just going to take his money. As far as the killing part, I didn't know this.

LONDON: Did you think that Doctor Sheppard would turn you in to the police after this robbery?

SMITH: I didn't.

LONDON: Why didn't you?

SMITH: Because Doc knew me for two years, and I knew that the doc, even knowing him, you know, the doc, you know, being with him, I was qualified to make money on my own, 'cause he ain't never had seen me really just down and out and broke. Sure he did me a favor, but he know that I was making money and I could make money. I shoot pool, I shoot dice, you know, and like I say, I was letting them make them some money. You know, I could make money myself, you know.

That's what Smith said, word for word, and he expected us to believe his story. In fact, he was *certain* we would believe him. He talked to us as if we were old friends.

Much still needed to be covered, but we had to be careful. There couldn't be even the suggestion of abuse. I asked Smith if he wanted a sandwich and soft drink (meals which a penny-pinching administration insisted detectives pay for), and when he said yes, I went to get them. Much as I disliked treating him to a meal, it beat hearing a defense lawyer saying I starved the confession out of him.

# • 12 •

AFTER all the speculation, frustration, and hard work, I felt like a man reborn hearing this sanitized, i.e., Candy-as-bystander eyewitness version of Dr. Sheppard's murder. We made sure Smith was ready to continue, then turned the tape recorder on again.

LONDON: All right. After Doctor Sheppard was killed, the body stayed in your apartment until after midnight. Is that correct?

SMITH: Uh-huh.

DILLMANN: I'd like to take this a little bit slower. John, you mentioned earlier in this statement that the doctor arrived at your home about nine o'-clock that morning.

SMITH: Uh-huh.

DILLMANN: So when he arrived that morning, who was at your apartment with you?

SMITH: Harold and Red.

DILLMANN: Red was your roommate, and the second subject's name is Harold Patin?

SMITH: Uh-huh.

DILLMANN: Would you give me a description of Harold Patin?

SMITH: Five-nine, weigh about one sixty, one sixty-five.

DILLMANN: Approximately how old is he?

SMITH: Twenty-six, twenty-five.

DILLMANN: Medium built, heavy built?

SMITH: Medium.

DILLMANN: Any hair on his face, goatee, moustache, anything like that?

SMITH: He have a little moustache.

DILLMANN: How does he wear his hair?

SMITH: Just combed, you know, just regular combed.

DILLMANN: Do you know where he lives?

SMITH: I do.

DILLMANN: Where is that, John?

SMITH: Lafitte Project.

DILLMANN: Do you know who he lives with?

SMITH: Some chick, I don't know the chick's name.

DILLMANN: Have you seen Harold since the doctor was killed?

SMITH: I seen him once or twice. I seen him about two weeks ago.

DILLMANN: Have you seen Red since the doc was killed?

SMITH: I done seen Red about twice, once in the pool hall. He said that he had got a job.

DILLMANN: Did he mention where he was working?

SMITH: He didn't.

DILLMANN: Okay, John, let's get back to the morning of January 20 when Doctor Sheppard arrived at your apartment. He knocked on your door, is that correct?

SMITH: Uh-huh.

DILLMANN: Who answered the door?

SMITH: The door was open. I said, come in.
DILLMANN: Where were you when you said come in?
SMITH: I was in the bedroom.
DILLMANN: That's the rear bedroom, is that correct?
SMITH: Uh-huh.
DILLMANN: What happened when Doctor Sheppard walked into your apartment?
SMITH: He came on straight to the bedroom. Spoke and started getting undressed.
DILLMANN: Where were Harold Patin and Red at that time?
SMITH: In the bathroom.
DILLMANN: You mentioned earlier that they had a pistol, is that correct?
SMITH: Uh-huh.
DILLMANN: Can you give me a description of this pistol?
SMITH: Well, the pistol was phony, it wasn't no real pistol. It wasn't no blank pistol, but it sounded like a blank pistol. It had a plug in the end, you know, like a little red plug in the end of a toy pistol. The pistol wasn't real, it was a little play gun.
DILLMANN: Now, as soon as the doctor got into your apartment, he took off his clothes?
SMITH: Uh-huh.
DILLMANN: What was Doctor Sheppard wearing that day, do you remember?
SMITH: A pair of, I think, gray pants . . . gray pants, and a shirt. He just pulled off his pants, and he said, I got to go to the bathroom.

He was right on the gray pants.

DILLMANN: All right, now, this is very important, John: Do you remember, when he took his pants off, did he have underwear on?

SMITH: Well, I didn't pay no attention, but I think he did. I'll say he did.

DILLMANN: What clothes did Doctor Sheppard have on when he walked into the bathroom?

SMITH: A shirt, a T-shirt, and socks.

Bingo! He was right on everything! *We have him,* I thought foolishly.

DILLMANN: Once he got to the bathroom, what happened?

SMITH: I heard the noise. I know that they was in there, you know, doing what they had planned to do. But I wanted to say before he went in there, because at the last minute, I still wanted to cop out from doing that and from even letting them rip him off. You know, I wanted to cop out then. I said, when he was going in the bathroom, you know, I wanted to say, well, hey doc, don't go in there, let's go somewhere else, you know, like that. But I didn't say nothing after I heard the tumbling.

DILLMANN: You heard the tumbling, you said?

SMITH: Right. I walked from the bedroom. I looked in there and he was laying on the floor.

DILLMANN: Did you go into the bathroom?

SMITH: I went to the kitchen. When I got to the kitchen I automatically see what was happening, you know.

DILLMANN: Where exactly was the doctor lying at that point?

SMITH: Across the floor. Half of his body was in the bathroom, and half was in the kitchen.

DILLMANN: Was he on his stomach?

SMITH: His stomach.

DILLMANN: And what were Red and Harold doing at that time?

SMITH: Well, Red was getting something to cover him with . . . to put on his body.

DILLMANN: He was still alive at that point, wasn't he?

SMITH: Yeah, he was. So they asked, you know, how much was it? There wasn't but forty dollars.

DILLMANN: How did you know about the money?

SMITH: How I know how much money the doc had?

DILLMANN: Yes.

SMITH: Well, they had left it, ah, you know, the doc had pulled off his pants in the room.

DILLMANN: Am I correct in assuming that while they grabbed the doctor in the bathroom and held him with the fake pistol, you went into the doctor's pants and removed the money? [*I guessed he missed the credit card.*]

SMITH: Well, I did.

DILLMANN: What did Harold and Red say?

SMITH: Nothing, but that it wasn't worth, you know, the while for them to, you know, to have robbed, because there wasn't no money. You know, they had did something that they didn't get no money or nothing out of it, and had taken a chance at getting some time.

DILLMANN: Now, you stated they mentioned that it wasn't worthwhile robbing him for forty dollars, and that they could get some heavy time for that, is that correct?

SMITH: Uh-huh.

DILLMANN: Is it, at that point, that they mentioned killing the doc?

SMITH: Well, not at that particular time. They stood there for a while, and everybody was wondering what they were going to do. Well, I was getting ready to leave myself, you know, like I was scared from the jump, you know.

DILLMANN: Did you give either Harold or Red the money at that point?

SMITH: I left it in the wallet. I just laid it back on the dresser. I didn't put it back in his pants. And I was standing in the other room, right there, so I could see in the kitchen door. So I was standing right there, and I was talking to them and they were saying, well, they had to dispose of him, and I was wondering what . . .

DILLMANN: They said they had to dispose of him?

SMITH: Right. And so, they didn't have nothing to kill him with. Like I said, his gun was, you know, that wasn't no real gun or nothing. And that's when they decided they had to strangle him. They didn't have nothing to strangle him with, so my radio was sitting there.

DILLMANN: Where, exactly, was the radio?

SMITH: It was on the table, the table just as you walk in the front door, you know, the table that sit there. I had it there with the cord plugged in the bottom. Red went and got the radio, and he just put one foot on it, and snapped the cord out. And then just wrapped it around the neck and he started pulling.

I had never felt surer of anything than this: Smith substituted Red for himself. Red—the guy he had lived with, but whose name he couldn't remember. Proving it would have to wait. Let Smith tell his story. He was doing a great job buying himself a first-degree murder rap.

DILLMANN: John, was just Red choking the doctor with the cord?

SMITH: Well, Red, he put the cord around the neck first to choke him, but apparently he didn't have enough strength to choke, and Harold grabbed the other end.

DILLMANN: Now let me get this down. Am I correct? What you're saying is that after you told them there was only forty dollars, then they wanted to dispose of the doctor because they didn't want to be identified, right?

SMITH: Right.

DILLMANN: Then Red went and pulled a cord out of your radio, wrapped it around the doctor's neck, and started to choke him, but he wasn't strong enough to do it, so Harold took one end of the cord. Is that correct?

SMITH: Uh-huh.

DILLMANN: Red took the other end of the cord, and they both pulled? Is that correct?

SMITH: That's correct.

I didn't believe it was. John Smith, not Red, held one end of that cord.

DILLMANN: Where were you standing?

SMITH: In the living room.

DILLMANN: You had clear view of what they were doing?

SMITH: Right.

DILLMANN: Is that how they killed the doctor, with that cord?

SMITH: Right, that's how.

DILLMANN: So, you witnessed the murder. You saw them both pull it?

SMITH: I saw them.

DILLMANN: About how long did it take to strangle him?

SMITH: Five or six minutes.

I believed him and tried to keep from shuddering. Five or six minutes would have been an eternity.

DILLMANN: What was the doctor doing while this was going on? Did he struggle at all, John?

SMITH: Yeah. After they started choking him, then you know, quite naturally, he started, you know, pulling. Then that's when Red, you know, sat on his leg and fought to put the cord on his foot.

LONDON: Was the doctor able to say anything? Did he scream for any help?

SMITH: He didn't scream.

LONDON: He didn't say a word at all?

SMITH: He didn't say anything.

LONDON: Did he appear scared to you?

SMITH: Well, really, he wasn't scared, I think, because, like I said, me and the doc had been knowing one another a long time, and he didn't feel that nothing was going to happen, 'cause he know that, I guess, you know, that I wouldn't do anything to him like that, to harm him. He really figured that they were just going to rob him, you know, probably then go head home.

DILLMANN: I see.

I did see. Sheppard didn't say anything because he had a sock shoved down his throat.

SMITH: And so, after he did struggle, after they put the cord around his neck, you know, he started struggling then.

DILLMANN: After they strangled the doctor, you mentioned they went and got a sheet?

SMITH: Uh-huh.

DILLMANN: What was the reason for getting the sheet?

SMITH: To cover him up.

DILLMANN: Can you describe the sheet to me in more detail than just being yellow? Anything else about it that you can remember?

SMITH: I think it's the one that covers the mattress. It got elastic on the thing.

DILLMANN: You're saying it was a fitted sheet?

SMITH: That's what it is.

DILLMANN: Who went and got that sheet?

SMITH: Red.

DILLMANN: And he wrapped the doctor in the sheet?

SMITH: Well, he put it up around from his shoulder to his head.

DILLMANN: Okay, now, the cord is already around the doctor's neck, then the sheet was around his head. Is that correct?

SMITH: Uh-huh.

DILLMANN: And the stocking?

SMITH: That was the first. . . . The stocking was to keep him from screaming.

DILLMANN: Before they strangled the doctor with the radio cord, they retrieved a pair of panty hose or stockings, and they put a sock in the doctor's mouth to keep him from screaming, is that correct?

SMITH: That's correct.

DILLMANN: Who got the panty hose?

SMITH: Well, the panty hose was already in the bathroom.

DILLMANN: Who did the panty hose belong to?

SMITH: My old lady.

DILLMANN: What is her name?

SMITH: Daisy Scott.

DILLMANN: Is that the woman whose home you were at when I picked you up?

SMITH: Right.

DILLMANN: So the sheet is around his head, the stocking is used as a gag, and the cord is around his neck, right? Did they use any other sheets?

SMITH: Nothing but a green trash bag.

DILLMANN: What did they do with that trash bag?

SMITH: Put it on his head, you know, just put it over him.

DILLMANN: Did they use any other sheets?

SMITH: Not to my remembering.

DILLMANN: So what happened next? The doctor is dead, they have him wrapped up in a sheet; they have the plastic bag over his head. Then what did you do?

SMITH: Well, I told them I was going home.

DILLMANN: John, you were home.

We had become a comedy act, and I didn't like it. He was so sure we had bought his incredible story that he felt he could say anything.

SMITH: Yeah, but what I was saying, I was getting away from there, I was leaving there. I was going to spend some time somewhere else. So I went on to my old lady and I laid there in the bed.

DILLMANN: You went over to Daisy's house?

SMITH: Uh-huh.

DILLMANN: Did you mention anything to Daisy?

SMITH: No, I didn't because I didn't want her to know that anything had went down. So I laid there till about ten or eleven o'clock. I say about twelve o'clock I got up and went to the project.

DILLMANN: John, when you left the apartment, you left Harold and Red there?

SMITH: Well, Red was getting ready to come outside with me, but Harold, he was running around up in there. I think he was looking for a little more money. He figured there was more than forty dollars.

DILLMANN: Who took the money, John?

SMITH: Ah, they split it up. It wasn't but forty dollars, they had twenty dollars apiece. They went and got speed, and Harold, I think he finally wound up to the project. I don't know where Red went.

He struck me as a pathetic liar: He got none of the money? And the murder couldn't have been more sordid. Worst of all, there wasn't a twinge of remorse, not now, and I doubted if there ever had been. No humanity at all. Sheppard's life had been squeezed out of him by people too desensitized even to question the deed.

DILLMANN: When did you next come back to the apartment?

SMITH: Well, I didn't come to the apartment. I went to the project where Harold live, and I was telling him about, you know, this lady that I dig, and that you know, I was welcome to, you know, come home and stay, 'cause that is home, you know. Come home and sleep. So, he said, I told him that, well, buddy, you know, you got to get this, this man's body out of here. And it's up to you all to get him out of here.

DILLMANN: All right, let's slow down a little bit. You were telling Harold or Red?

SMITH: I was telling Harold.

DILLMANN: You were telling Harold that he had to get the doctor's body out of your apartment so you could go sleep?

SMITH: Right.

DILLMANN: What was his reaction to that?

SMITH: He said, bro, I am a do it, he said, but, you know, you know we got to get a ride. So I said, bro, you have to get one now, you know. So, he met, well it wasn't really then, it was later that night.

DILLMANN: This was Friday night, January twentieth? About what time would you say it was when you were talking to Harold about getting rid of the body?

SMITH: Oh, about eight-thirty or something to nine, something like that.

DILLMANN: Did you, in fact, find someone with a car?

SMITH: Well, like I say, he had a partner with a car. So, he borrowed his car, but it wasn't right then, it was later that night.

DILLMANN: About what time?

SMITH: Oh, one or two.

DILLMANN: One or two in the morning. So that would be one or two on Saturday morning?

SMITH: Right.

DILLMANN: Do you know who Harold Patin borrowed the car from? Do you know the gentleman's name?

SMITH: Ah, wait, now, he was another one that we call Red.

DILLMANN: He was another Red.

SMITH: Yeah, but he got a lot of hair. I don't think he had knew why he was lending his car, you know, 'cause I had asked, I said, bro, I said, the car, I said, the dude know what you gonna do with the car? He said no, but he said I just got it, he said I got to return it back in an hour or so, he said, but he don't know nothing.

DILLMANN: Can you give me a description of this car?

SMITH: Chevrolet, white, sixty-three or sixty-four, something like that.

DILLMANN: Then you and Harold went back to the apartment?

SMITH: Uh-huh.

DILLMANN: Red wasn't with you?

SMITH: No.

DILLMANN: When you went back upstairs, the doctor's body was in the same position?

SMITH: Uh-huh.

DILLMANN: John, this is important. Was there any blood at that time in the bathroom?

SMITH: There was blood, you know, wasted over the bathroom, but I don't know where it had come from, but it was there.

DILLMANN: Do you think possibly it might have come from the doctor?

SMITH: It had to. There wasn't nobody else it could have come from.

I'm not making up this dialogue, and I find it frightening that there are *so many* John Smiths out there.

DILLMANN: Was it a lot of blood, John?

SMITH: It was.

The blood, of course, had come from that "trauma to the right temple." Dr. McGarry said Sheppard had "bled profusely" from the right ear.

DILLMANN: The blood was on the floor? In the bathroom?

SMITH: Uh-huh.

DILLMANN: So you and Harold took the doctor's body out, is that correct?

SMITH: Right.

DILLMANN: You took it down the steps?

SMITH: Uh-huh.

DILLMANN: Who carried the doctor's head?

SMITH: Patin.

DILLMANN: And what did you carry?

SMITH: The feet.

DILLMANN: All right, now this is very important, John. Listen to me. At any time during the course of going down the steps into the alleyway, did you bump up against that wall?

SMITH: We stopped on the step, the first step, you know, just coming around it, we stopped right there. That was the only stop.

DILLMANN: To your knowledge, was there any blood dripping from the doctor?

SMITH: No.

DILLMANN: Do you think you might have brushed up against the wall coming down the steps with the doctor's body. Is that possible?

SMITH: It's possible, yeah.

And that's where the bloody handprint came from.

DILLMANN: Now, the doctor's upper torso was covered with the sheet and the plastic bag. Is that correct?

SMITH: Right.

DILLMANN: What about his legs? Was the rest of his body covered with anything?

SMITH: Yeah, it was.

DILLMANN: What was it covered with, John?

SMITH: Sheet.

DILLMANN: What color sheet?

SMITH: Well, it got to be white. There wasn't another yellow one. It had to be white.

DILLMANN: What about the rest of the doctor's clothes?

SMITH: I think they all was in the bag.

DILLMANN: So, you're saying the doctor's clothing was put in the plastic bag that was put over the doctor's head, and then the rest of his body was wrapped in a white sheet, and you and Harold Patin carried the body down the stairwell to the alleyway and then out to the Chevrolet?

SMITH: Right.

DILLMANN: Did you put the body in the trunk or inside the car?

SMITH: In the inside.

DILLMANN: The backseat?

SMITH: Uh-huh.

DILLMANN: On the floor?

SMITH: Uh-huh.

DILLMANN: Who drove the car?

SMITH: Patin.

DILLMANN: And you rode on the passenger side, correct? How did you determine what to do with the body?

SMITH: Well, I didn't determine. He determined to take it to the dump. I didn't know where the dump was. He just picked a spot and that was it.

DILLMANN: Where did you dump the body?

SMITH: On the side, I don't know the name of the street. It's on the side of the road, somewhere, you know, off from the dump.

DILLMANN: On the side of the road out by the dump? Is that what you're saying?

SMITH: Yeah. It's not the dump, but, you know, it's the road going to the dump.

DILLMANN: The road that goes to the dump. Could that be Almonaster?

SMITH: It could be.

DILLMANN: Is that out in New Orleans East, out in the Seventh District, out toward . . .

SMITH: Going out toward the main waters.

DILLMANN: Right, on the lake?

SMITH: Yeah.

DILLMANN: Now, why did you decide to stop there?

SMITH: We just picked a location.

DILLMANN: And then you and Harold—I don't want to put words in your mouth—but then you and Harold took the body out of the car?

SMITH: Right.

DILLMANN: And dumped it? Is that correct?

SMITH: Right.

DILLMANN: What did you do next?

SMITH: Got in the car and drove on. I came back home. I laid down and went to sleep, and he came over that morning and helped clean up.

DILLMANN: Who came over that morning?

SMITH: Harold.

DILLMANN: Did you see Red?

SMITH: Not right then. I seen Red about a week afterward.

DILLMANN: What did you do in the apartment to clean up?

SMITH: Nothing but mop the blood up.

DILLMANN: You mopped the blood up?

SMITH: Well, it wasn't really mopping. We did it with some towels.

DILLMANN: And what did you do with the bloody towels?

SMITH: Just put them in a trash bag and sent them to the dump.

DILLMANN: John, since Doctor Sheppard has been killed, have you and Red and Harold discussed the murder at all?

SMITH: No.

DILLMANN: It's just been completely forgotten about?

SMITH: Uh-huh.

LONDON: John, can you read and write?

SMITH: No.

LONDON: Do you have any problem understanding what we're saying?

SMITH: I don't.

LONDON: Are you on any medication right now that would prevent you from fully understanding what we're doing?

SMITH: No.

LONDON: You are aware, aren't you, that the entire conversation is being taped?

SMITH: I am.

LONDON: And this information was given freely and voluntarily?

SMITH: It was.

DILLMANN: John, why have you made this statement? For what reason?

SMITH: I guess my conscience.

DILLMANN: Has it bothered you, John?

SMITH: It has. My old lady could tell something was bothering me, but she ain't never know what it was.

LONDON: And nobody promised you anything in exchange for your statement?

SMITH: No. Nobody promised me nothing.

When the interview concluded, I took Smith to the medical examiner's office a block away and had Dr. Monroe Samuels examine him and photograph him, from head to foot, for bruises. It was a precaution I'd adopted very early in my homicide career. The defense attorney was *guaranteed* to claim that the confession had been beaten out of him.

I thought we had John Smith wrapped into a neat little package. There would still be plenty of work to do tying Patin and perhaps the two Reds into the murder and its aftermath, but Candy, I genuinely believed, had condemned himself.

# • 13 •

SMITH was in high spirits as he guided us around New Orleans. He seemed to view himself as a hero, a good citizen who solved homicides. No, more than that: Seated in the unmarked car I drove at his direction, it was as if he were a fellow cop. He chatted easily, almost intimately, like a good friend might, one close pal to a pair of his buddies. Frequently he used the word "we" when talking about bringing Patin and Red to justice, and I thought I would retch.

It was too bad about Dr. Sheppard, Candy conceded, but now that he, John Smith, had "come forward," justice could take its course. He didn't display a single doubt that we had swallowed his story hook, line, and sinker. I listened to his patter, because he could still help us, but when he asked about my family, I almost lost my grip.

Candy's guided tour came right after we left the photographing session at the coroner's office. First we drove to 1127 Touro Street, his current residence. We needed to ascertain the address to obtain a search warrant: Smith could find his home, but he didn't know the street number.

Why should I be surprised? He had lived a considerable time with someone he knew only as Red.

Next Candy showed us 619 North Miro Street, the address of Harold Patin's girlfriend. We intended to obtain a murder warrant for Patin's arrest. I *suspected* he and Smith had choked the life from Dr. Sheppard, and believed we would learn the exact truth. Candy had already turned rat: The others should be eager to provide their versions.

Smith talked about his pool hustling coups, a variety of other scams, even his skills as a lover of women. "They won't leave me alone." It occurred to me as he chattered on that this heterosexual male prostitute who serviced homosexuals would probably do anything except work.

I seldom have found a killer I might like under different circumstances, but generally an acquired professional detachment prevented me from actively loathing the subject. I couldn't help myself with John Smith, this never-give-it-another-thought hustler who now believed himself a friend. What grated on me the most, I think, was his seeming heartfelt conviction that he possessed superior intelligence, genuine savoir faire, when in reality, by any measurement, he ranked very high on an ignorance scale.

Or was he just putting us on? Did he *pretend* that he thought we believed him? I don't think so. By God, I imagined him thinking, I've put one over on these dumb detectives.

By the time we returned to police headquarters, word was out and so was the media. TV cameras recorded John Smith, flanked by London and me, taking what had been dubbed the Hollywood Walk, the paved path linking the station with Central Lockup.

Candy expressed surprise and anger that we weren't letting him go. He acted as if we had betrayed him. "I told you, man," he said, "I didn't kill the doc."

"John," I said. "Not that it makes any difference. But I think you were on one end of that cord."

Back in the office I asked Big Hector to fill out an application for a search warrant for Touro Street. Then I punched Harold Patin into the computer and got data on our second murder suspect: black, listed address 3000 LaSalle Street, apartment 21, age 27, 5′10″, 150 pounds, nickname "Blue."

What fascinated me about Patin was a different sort of vital statistics—his arrest record. Patin fit the definition of career criminal: eleven felony busts, three felony convictions.

He had been released from Angola State Prison in September 1977, after serving six years for armed robbery. In the four months after his release and Sheppard's murder, he had been charged with *seven* additional felonies.

This document recording a virtual one-man crime wave told me that Patin was capable of standing on Sheppard's throat and pulling on the cord.

I needed sleep but couldn't take any, because Patin needed only to turn on his TV to learn of Candy's arrest and the desirability of making himself scarce.

London, Baumy, Egan, and I went to 3000 LaSalle Street, not far from Headquarters, prepared to hit the place hard. Each of us carried a shotgun, two going to the front door and two to the back, but the place was deserted. We located Patin's landlord, but he had no idea where his former tenant had moved.

Next we journeyed to 619 North Miro, which Candy had pointed out as the residence of Patin's girlfriend. Cynthia McCants talked to us on her front porch.

"I haven't seen Blue for two or three months," she said. "He could be anywhere, maybe even in jail."

He wasn't, though. I checked. I figured if he hadn't previously gone underground to dodge those seven felony charges, he had done it now, with the news of Smith's arrest on the street.

"What about his family?" I asked Cynthia McCants. "Where does his mother stay?"

"In St. Thomas Project. I don't know the address."

"Do you mind if I take a look inside?" He might be there, but more likely we would find his clothes.

We made a walkthrough. Nothing.

And that's about what I had left. I found the energy to send out a teletype (an arrest and wanted bulletin) to all the divisions and districts in the department. This announced the arrest of Candy, and that Patin, armed and dangerous, was wanted for the same murder and should be approached with extreme caution.

The sun was going down when I pointed the car toward sparkling Lake Pontchartrain and home.

We found the radio the next day. Not at Smith's Touro Street address—Big Hector's search of that apartment came up empty—but at Daisy Scott's home, entered with a second search warrant. It was a small, green clock radio with a new cord attached, and Daisy stated that it belonged to Candy. A subsequent check with Kawasaki dealers confirmed that the cord around Dr. Sheppard's neck could have come from this radio.

The gods smiled on me this March 10. Not only did we find the appliance from which the murder weapon likely had been torn, but we got a break that added frosting to our already lavishly decorated prosecutorial cake.

His name was Alton "Red" Tumblin, and he called Homicide about noon after reading in the *Times-Picayune* about John Smith's arrest. Tumblin lived at 2510 Dumaine, a residential section near Armstrong Park, and said he knew John Smith and Harold Patin. Before he could go any further, I said, "Hold on. Let me come out to see you."

I brought Big Hector along because it simply wasn't

good policy for anyone—even a cop—to roam around that neighborhood alone. Tumblin, twenty-eight, met us on his front porch and let us into a nicely furnished living room. We were about to hear a remarkable story.

"Alton," I said, "I'm handling the Sheppard murder investigation. I understand you have some information."

"Like I told you, I saw on the news where Candy's been arrested for the killing, and I hear on the street that you're looking for Harold Patin."

"That's true. Do you know where I can find him?"

"No. But I'll tell you what. I think those two dudes used my car to dump the doctor's body."

"Your car? Were you there?"

"Hell, no. But I need to straighten this out. Harold borrowed my car one night. He was supposed to use it for an hour, but he kept it all night. Then yesterday I see Harold's old lady, Cynthia, and she tells me not to tell the police about Harold borrowing the car. Man, when I saw on the news that Candy got busted, and the body dumped in that swamp, I put two and two together. To make matters worse, Harold and Candy run with this dude called Red. They call me Red. I don't need no mistaken identity. I want this straightened out right now."

"You say Patin borrowed your car and kept it all night?"

"Yeah. The whole night."

"When was this?"

"On a Friday in January. I looked it up after I called you. It was January twentieth. He didn't bring it back until Saturday morning."

January 21. The morning Smith said they had taken Sheppard's body out to Almonaster.

"Did Patin say why he wanted the car?"

"No. Just that he needed it for an hour. I did him a favor, and now I'm afraid I'm in trouble."

"Where's the car now?"

Tumblin got up and pointed out the window to a white 1964 Chevy parked on the street. "That's it right there."

"How long have you known Harold Patin?"

"A good while. He ran me into his friend Candy, and this guy Red I was telling you about. I mostly see them when we shoot dice at Patin's house on Miro Street."

"What about this other Red? Can you describe him to me?"

"He lived with Candy for a while. He's just a kid. About eighteen years old, tall, skinny, real light skin."

"Do you know his real name, or where he lives now?"

"No. They just call him Red."

"Exactly what did Cynthia McCants say about the car?"

"She came over yesterday, all nervous. She told me, like I said, not to tell the police I'd lent my car to Harold. I tried to find out why, but she wouldn't say. When I learned Harold was wanted for this murder, I figured it out."

"Alton," I said, getting to my feet, "let's take a look at your car."

We went outside, opened the trunk just in case, but saw no obvious stains. Well, he hadn't been in the trunk, according to Candy. We looked in the backseat, where Sheppard had been, but I couldn't spot anything.

"Alton," I said, "I'm going to need you to come to Headquarters and give me a statement. Why don't you follow us in your car?"

"Sure. I want this cleared up."

I felt a little guilty not telling him that we would impound the Chevrolet as soon as he arrived at Headquarters. NOPD's "taxi service" would bring him home.

We simply had to have this vehicle. The crime lab technicians would process the entire car: photograph, dust for prints, scour for blood, hair, fibers (from a yellow sheet, Sheppard's clothes)—a millimeter-by-millimeter search.

We took a detailed sworn statement from Tumblin, locking him into what he had told us. No way could he convincingly change his story, nor was there any indication he would want to do that. Then I drove this star witness home.

Tumblin wasn't happy about losing his car, albeit temporarily (though we might keep it all the way through the trial), but his fear—real indeed—of being pulled into the murder made him cooperative. I kept praising him as a fine citizen, which was true, and promised to do everything I could to get his car back speedily.

I suppose I've had other days as good as this one, but I can't remember any. I hadn't been at my desk ten minutes before Tumblin was back on the phone.

"Detective Dillmann?" he asked.

I figured he wanted to complain about being without wheels.

"What can I do for you, Alton?"

"You know that dude Red, Candy's roommate?"

"What about him? Did you find out his name?"

"No. But I got him."

"What do you mean you got him?"

"I was on the way to my mother's house, and I saw him on the corner. I talked to him and tried to get his name, and when I told him what this was about, he said he wanted to speak to you."

He did? Candy had said that this Red, Red II (Tumblin I labeled Red I), had stood on one end of that electrical cord, Patin on the other, and spent "five or six minutes" choking the life out of Dr. Sheppard.

"Where is he now?"

"Standing right next to me."

"Where are you?"

"At the intersection of Lafitte and Rocheblave."

"Don't move. I'll be there in ten minutes."

* * *

I interviewed Red II, real name Wendell Blanks, age seventeen, in the same room where the previous day I had taken John Smith's confession. Blanks was tall and very thin, just a kid, and before I talked to him I checked and learned he had no arrest record whatever. This didn't fit the profile of a savage strangler.

I read Blanks his rights, adding that he was a suspect in Dr. Sheppard's murder, and he interrupted to ask who Dr. Sheppard was.

"Wendell," I said, "do you know John Smith? They call him Candy."

"Sure. I used to live with him."

"When was that?"

"Last year."

"Can you be more specific?"

"I moved in about early November, and he threw me out before Christmas. Must have been the first part of December. I lost my job and couldn't pay my half of the rent. He let me stay a few days, but I couldn't find another job right away, and he said I had to leave."

"What kind of work do you do?"

"Anything. I was a laborer. Worked for a construction company. It's tough to get a job. You work for a while, then the job's over, and they lay you off."

"Are you gay, Wendell?"

"What's gay? I don't understand."

This young man hadn't killed anybody. He belonged in high school, not on the streets.

"Homosexual," I said. "You know, do you like guys?"

"Hell, no. I'm all man. Do I look like a sissy?"

I thought about John Smith, the muscular streetwise Candy, and Harold Patin, with his lengthy felony arrest ledger, and then this youngster, a J.J. Walker look-alike from the TV sitcom "Good Times." Wendell Blanks hadn't killed anyone, in my opinion.

"What about Candy? Is he a sissy?"

"I don't think so. He has a girlfriend named Daisy. She would come and visit. Look, what did Candy say I did, Lieutenant?"

I let the promotion pass.

"Candy said you killed Doctor Sheppard," I said.

Surprise spread instantly across his face. He pursed his lips and let out a long, low whistle. "Look, I ain't killed nobody in my life. I heard Candy talk about some doctor friend of his who had a lot of money. I don't even know his name."

"Wendell, are you positive you moved out of that apartment on Marais in December? Couldn't it have been in January?"

"I'm positive. It was weeks before Christmas. I can prove it."

He'd have to. More important, I believed he hadn't killed Dr. Sheppard. I hated what I had to do to this innocent kid, something much worse than taking Tumblin's car.

"How can you prove it?"

"I moved back in with my mama. She can tell you."

"Wendell, listen closely. Have you and Candy had any kind of falling out? An argument? A fight?"

"No. I still see him on the street. He waves when he sees me."

"Then, why in the world would John Smith name you as the murderer, and say he saw you kill Doctor Sheppard?"

"He probably done it himself. Now he's blaming it on me to get out of the rap."

A budding detective, I thought. Maybe NOPD should recruit him in a few years.

I looked at Blanks neutrally. Damn! Few things ranked

worse for a detective than delivering this sort of bad news.

"Wendell, I'm sorry I have to tell you this. But, first, I want you to know I believe you, that I don't think you had anything to do with Doctor Sheppard's murder. Nevertheless, I'm going to have to book you for it."

"You say you believe me? And you're going to arrest me anyway?"

"I don't have a choice." I really didn't. I told him I was sorry—poor consolation—but that Candy's confession implicating him in murder left me without an option.

"How long will I have to stay in jail?" Tears welled in his eyes.

"I won't lie to you, Wendell. Probably a couple of weeks."

"What can I tell my mother?"

"Tell her I don't think you're guilty. That all this will get worked out. I can't imagine the grand jury indicting you just on Candy Smith's word. Listen, let me offer some advice: Make very sure you find people who can document that you moved out of that apartment long before January."

"Lieutenant, this grand jury. Will you talk for me? Take my side? Make them understand Candy's lying on me?"

"Positively, Wendell. Not only the grand jury, but the district attorney, too."

I kept my word. I talked to Assistant District Attorney Joe Meyer, who had been assigned the case right after we took Smith's confession. He agreed we should spring Blanks from jail the moment we could, and that the remaining loose end was the capture of Harold Patin.

# • 14 •

WARNING signs began to appear, in the form of little things going wrong, usually routine matters becoming high barriers. For example, Mr. "No Problem" Dick Price, his voice filled with frustration, reported that he hadn't learned Sheppard's blood type.

"It's unbelievable," Price told me on the phone from Florida. "I've checked the doc's medical history from childhood to college to St. Anthony's—zero. I can't find his blood type anywhere. I'm telling you, John, it's as if he was never sick."

"Childhood?" For a moment I felt uneasy. A bit guilty, I suppose. Questions about growing-up years had never arisen, and I hadn't bothered to check.

"Yeah. He came from upstate New York. Adored his mother, not too fond of his father, that sort of arrangement. Father was a geologist. Mother wrote books. The mother died many years ago—Sheppard talked about her a lot—the father not too long ago. Of course, the doc was an only child."

I wondered about his mother, the book writer, and later checked her out. Her two published works, one about North Carolina, the other Pennsylvania, were, of course, out of print, but for a short time they had created a stir. The people she wrote about took umbrage at the way she characterized them: Mrs. Sheppard evidently had been a woman who admired grace and culture, qualities she found lacking in her subjects. Surely, I thought, it had been her influence that instilled a love of beautiful objects in her son.

Price had been detailing his efforts to locate Sheppard's blood type. "I'm about tapped out," he concluded, "and it's a real bummer not being able to find something that's so common."

"It's bound to be on file somewhere," I said confidently. "Don't worry about it. I've got a few places I can check here."

But a few days later, after learning no blood type had been recorded at his alma mater, LSU Medical School, or at Charity Hospital where he interned, I had a better feel for Price's bewilderment.

It didn't seem to me that learning Sheppard's blood type should be any tougher than finding a good bowl of gumbo in the French Quarter. Everybody, I told myself, had their blood type recorded somewhere. As soon as indictments were handed down—they were expected in a week—it wouldn't be my job to worry about it; the case would officially be out of my hands.

Unofficially, it already was. I had given all my evidence to Assistant District Attorney Joe Meyer, and his investigators (police officers assigned full-time to the prosecutor) now had the job of preparing the case for trial. They were responsible for any loose ends, plus a good deal of thankless work such as making sure all witnesses were available to testify when needed. Although I would have to testify in front of the grand jury, and be a major witness at any trials, my work on this case had, for all practical purposes, ended. There were other murderers to nail.

Of course, it didn't completely work out that way. This

investigation had captivated me from the beginning, become my child, so to speak, and one doesn't cease to care because a child grows up and moves away.

The DA's investigators had no better luck with Sheppard's blood type than Price or I, despite serious outlay of manpower and money. It was no small matter; learning that the doctor's blood was Type B would match it to the sample found in the McKnight apartment, and help corroborate that Sheppard had been murdered there. Still, we already had what I considered unassailable corroboration: the details in Candy's tape-recorded statement that only a participant could know.

Another fly in the ointment was our inability to collar Harold Patin. Adding his name and physical description to the NCIC computer wanted list guaranteed attention from law officers across the country, and on the local scene finding him had become a top priority. Every cop in New Orleans knew kudos awaited the one who grabbed Patin, but increasingly it seemed we chased a shadow.

From a public-safety standpoint, I would have preferred having Harold Patin in custody rather than John Smith. Acquaintances described Patin as a fearsome individual, and reluctantly spoke about his short-fuse temper that often exploded in an ugly confrontation. Patin was a hardcore tough guy. His criminal record attested to a violent life background, and the armed-robbery conviction proved he would carry a weapon. How far would he go, I wondered, to avoid the electric chair, or prison doors slamming behind him for the rest of his life?

Informants, comfortable in the same tough environment where Harold Patin moved, kept their eyes peeled and ears open in the projects. Wanted posters plastered Patin's picture all over New Orleans and surrounding parishes. But we didn't get a lead, nothing. Several times a week I staked out the home of his girlfriend, Cynthia McCants, hoping lightning would strike.

I agreed with Joe Meyer's master plan. Since Patin didn't seem the sort to bare his soul, as Candy had, he intended to convict John Smith, using his confession and the damning testimony of Alton "Red" Tumblin (Red I, who loaned the car that transported Sheppard's body). Facing the electric chair, Meyer believed, Candy would then be more than willing to testify against his pal Patin in exchange for whatever he could get.

Little things. Alarm bells. The crime lab report on Alton Tumblin's car: Minute specks of blood were found on the floor of the backseat, but not enough to type.

In the same "little things" category, we learned Candy had found himself an alibi. Girlfriend Daisy Scott, who had mimed me right to his bathroom hiding place, had a change of heart. Now she swore that John Smith had spent most of January 20, including the critical murder hours, at her apartment.

I couldn't imagine even the most gullible juror swallowing this story. We had that confession, earned fairly after *four* Miranda warnings, very hard to beat in court: It was a hand roughly equivalent to four aces. Smith himself had admitted to witnessing the murder, not by closed-circuit television at Daisy Scott's apartment, but live, from just a few feet away. He mentioned going to Daisy's place only after the deed was done. I believed that by his own words, preserved on tape, Candy had tied himself a sturdy hangman's noose and now tried desperately to unravel the rope.

Through the jailhouse grapevine we heard what John Smith planned to claim in court: We had beaten the confession out of him. It was déjà vu all over again.

When Steve London and I were closeted in the interrogation room with our suspect on March 9, it didn't take many responses from the functionally illiterate Candy to convince us that we weren't questioning a rocket scientist. On the other hand, I had told myself, he had to possess a certain creativity to survive in the Quarter on pure hustle. Well, I had been wrong. After several days in the slammer putting his imagination to work, he hadn't come up with anything original, just that old standby, "They beat the shit out of me."

Well, we'd had him examined by Dr. Monroe Samuels right after the interrogation. The muscular Smith had been the very picture of good health. A short time later TV cameras recorded his Hollywood Walk. He had looked in better shape and a lot more alert than I did. He hadn't been pulling double and triple shifts.

Regardless, I know of no homicide detective who ever took a confession—and had the case go to court—who *didn't* get accused of brutality.

On March 28, 1978, I testified in front of the Orleans Parish Grand Jury, which handed down a first-degree murder indictment against John Smith. The grand jury, at the urging of Joe Meyer and myself, refused to indict seventeen-year-old Wendell Blanks, and he was released from custody.

Despite the pinpricks—not finding Harold Patin's or Sheppard's blood types—Joe Meyer and I felt the case against Candy was nearly airtight. Although we felt he had pulled on one end of the cord that choked the life from the St. Petersburg anesthesiologist, he had confessed to something equally serious in the eyes of the law: He was, in his own words, the participant in a crime where the result was murder.

Meyer and I had several lengthy sessions (I kept checking

on the prosecution's progress), and he occasionally enjoyed playing devil's advocate. It was a way for him to test his case on someone else.

"John," Meyer said to me, "a defense attorney is going to demand corroboration of this confession."

I loved this extracurricular part of the job. "Corroboration, huh?" I said, and wound myself up. "I'll give you corroboration. John Smith says Doctor Sheppard came to his apartment the morning of the murder. We know from the diaries that Sheppard had been there before. Smith said the doctor stripped down to his underwear before the killing. That's how we found the body clothed: in shorts and a T-shirt."

I looked at the veteran Meyer. His face was unreadable. Fine. I was into the game. "Smith says Sheppard's head was wrapped in a yellow bedsheet. True. He says the doctor was strangled with an electrical cord. True. He says a sock was shoved down Sheppard's throat. True."

Meyer still hadn't moved. His fingertips touched together beneath his chin, as if in prayer.

"How can Smith know all this information?" I continued. "Will the defense claim he's psychic? We never released any of it to the press. But let me go on. Smith says Sheppard was killed in the bathroom. We found human blood, plenty of it, right where it was supposed to be, in that bathroom. Smith says Patin borrowed a car from Red Tumblin and that he and Patin dumped the body off Almonaster. Patin did indeed borrow that car, and we found Sheppard where Candy said he'd be. Everything Smith told us fits the physical facts, and except for the location of the corpse, none of it was made public."

I didn't feel comfortable doing all the talking. But once again a pause had elicited no response from Meyer, so I carried it to the finish.

"Candy said the body was carried down the stairwell. We found a blood trail on the stairwell." I leaned back and looked at Meyer. "You wanted corroboration," I said. "I don't see how we could have much more."

Meyer nodded his head slowly. He had just wanted someone to confirm the way he viewed the case. Like a good detective, he needed to be certain the logic stood as nearly foolproof as possible. And I suspect there was more: District attorneys keep track of their win/lose stats as carefully as any baseball pitcher, using them in inner-circle competition to determine who racks up the best percentage of convictions versus acquittals. Much like athletic directors judge a coach by his victories and defeats, so does the DA evaluate his prosecutors. Not just the DA, either. Outside law firms look at the records these men build in office, so career advancement can be at stake.

Some prosecutors wonder, why handle an iffy case when so many easy pickings exist to keep the winning percentage up?

Actually, it's not always the worst way to reason. While it may lead to overzealousness, more often this prudence means prosecutors prosecute only when they believe they have proof "beyond a reasonable doubt."

Homicide detectives do not display their records so publicly, like chalked scores I've seen displayed in the DA's office, but in their heads they, too, know how they stand. I certainly did. Of my almost one hundred homicides that had so far gone to trial, I had "lost" only one. The case involved a fifteen-year-old paperboy having an affair with a middle-aged housewife. Somehow the youngster had reasoned that by murdering the husband he would achieve a lifetime of bliss with his true love. The boy had no history of criminal behavior and, I believe, because the state tried him as an adult and asked for life imprisonment, the jury acquitted rather than impose such a harsh sentence.

I don't know. I wonder if I might have voted the same way myself.

Anyway, John "Candy" Smith was far removed from that lovestruck paperboy. I believed him a remorseless, cold-blooded killer, and Joe Meyer intended to prosecute him as such.

The first preliminary hearing took place on May 12, Judge Matthew Braniff presiding. In the massive courtroom with its thirty-foot-high vaultlike ceiling and space for several hundred spectators, we learned that John Smith still rode a lucky streak. Not the it-happens-to-everybody-sometime luck of finding a ten-dollar bill on the sidewalk, but *big-time* fortune, like scoring as the sole winner of the Florida lottery.

Smith's lagniappe came in the form of a 5′8″ bundle of energy and brains named Arthur A. "Buddy" Lemann III, his court-appointed defense lawyer. Lemann (pronounced "Lemon," which he definitely wasn't), thirty-six, ranked among the finest criminal lawyers in New Orleans. Currently he was fresh from a victory in one of the most publicized cases in Louisiana history: the fraud trial of Dr. Joe Beasley, then dean of Tulane's School of Public Health and Tropical Medicine, accused of bribing a public official to support a birth-control program the doctor advocated as a means of reducing poverty. The Rockefeller and Ford Foundations were unindicted co-conspirators in the case, and Lemann, calling Dr. Beasley a "visionary," a "revolutionary," and a "great humanitarian," boldly offered to serve any sentence the medical man received.

It was typical of the flamboyant lawyer, and any prosecutor who went against him knew he faced a no-holds-barred fight to the finish.

Lemann, a graduate of Loyola Law School and an acclaimed scholar in constitutional law, served as a professor at his alma mater and headed its legal clinic. So, in the trial of John Smith, the state would be doing battle with this formidable opponent *plus* practically the entire senior law class at Loyola, which made him doubly and triply effective.

The Loyola Law School Clinic had the unique distinction of being the country's *only* university public-defender program that handled felonies, and was super-funded. It received abundant government money and generous endowments from the same Rockefeller and Ford Foundations that had backed Dr. Beasley. Buddy Lemann called it "the greatest program Louisiana ever had."

Maybe. But for certain the Clinic's entrance into the arena transformed a rather cut-and-dried case (after all, we had Smith's confession) into a clash of the titans. One of the primary arguments of civil libertarians protesting capital punishment is that the death penalty swallows up the economically disadvantaged—a point graphically illustrated by the fact that no truly wealthy person has ever been executed in the United States. A major reason for this is the extraordinary legal talent a rich defendant can hire to get him off the hook.

I don't believe a J. Paul Getty could have assembled a more awesome defense team than John Smith had handed to him by the luck of the draw—the Loyola Law School Clinic's name just happened to be at the top of the list when Candy's case was called. Every needy street-smart criminal in the city tried to arrange representation from Buddy Lemann's clinic, but it always came down to that roster of lawyers, and whose turn it was, a method very similar to how homicide detectives drew their investigations.

Lemann, later instrumental in securing the release from prison of reputed Mafia godfather Carlos Marcello (alleged by some to be connected to the John F. Kennedy assassination), would be described by *Mafia Kingfish* author John H.

Davis as "colorful and eloquent," a man who delivered absolutely brilliant closing arguments. To the latter I could attest: Buddy assumed the legal prowess of Clarence Darrow reincarnated when he stood to face a jury with his client's life at stake.

But Joe Meyer and I knew it wasn't just Lemann. He had a whole senior class at his beck and call: eager, fresh-faced, tireless young researchers chomping at the bit to impress their awe-inspiring professor. They were new at this game, full of courage, idealism, ethics, and optimism. More important, they had enthusiasm, will-to-win, and approached the case with the vigor of Holy Roman Empire crusaders. I couldn't help wondering how many of these firebrands the gristmill of time, politics, and dirty deals would slowly chew up and spit out as cynical, beaten-down aging public defenders, merely going through the motions. At any rate, today the budding barristers intended to show Professor Lemann they had the right stuff!

Conversely, Lemann, the teacher, didn't want to lose a case (and face?) in front of all these young men and women. His purpose was to show them how to win, not how to take defeat gracefully.

Candy had a virtual army working on his behalf, gung-ho soldiers directed by a winning general of vast cunning and skill.

Well, we weren't chopped liver. And for lovers of good courtroom drama, the John Smith trial promised to be among the best. Prosecutor Joe Meyer, thirty-nine, a New Orleans native and Tulane Law School grad, had no peer in the District Attorney's office. After graduating law school in 1969, he headed a legal services program for the poor, spent a year with a prestigious Philadelphia law firm, and joined DA Harry Connick's staff in 1975.

"Meteoric" best describes his rise as a prosecutor. In 1977 he was named Chief of Trials, a prized position second only to the district attorney. Meyer, a troubleshooter, had his pick of cases and handled only heaters, the ones guaranteed to attract controversy and press attention. He was awarded the title Special Prosecutor, and earned the reputation of not only winning cases, but *demolishing* the opposition. At 5′9″, an inch taller than Buddy Lemann, he smoked strong cigars Pascal Saladino would have approved of, and was extremely aggressive in court: A rough, no-nonsense lawyer who aimed straight for the jugular.

From a detective's point of view, the case couldn't have drawn a better advocate than Joe Meyer. He had no doubt of John Smith's guilt, and intended to prove it, no matter what rabbits Buddy Lemann pulled from his hat.

When the bailiff called this first preliminary hearing to order, I had to look several times before I recognized the defendant. Good thing Meyer isn't banking on eyewitness identification, I thought. The spiffy John Smith I saw sitting in the dock bore little resemblance to the roguish hustler the French Quarter poolhall set called Candy. The accused—clad in a fashionable blue suit, clean shaven, hair neatly trimmed, shoes polished to a Marine drill instructor's satisfaction—blended in so well with others seated at the defense table that I had mistaken him for one of Buddy Lemann's Class of '78 (plenty of these buzzed around). It turned out the law students had chipped in and bought Smith a new wardrobe. And Lemann's legion had done more than crack the law books for the defendant; they were coaching Candy on proper speech and etiquette, though I didn't learn this until months later when he took the stand at his trial.

Right away I did get treated to what a major portion of

Buddy Lemann's defense would be: A claim Steve London and I had beaten the confession from his client, that we had pummeled him savagely with our fists, including vicious blows with a blackjack to the groin, and ripped whiskers out of his chin with our fingernails.

I don't think for a moment Buddy Lemann believed any of these accusations of brutality. I *knew* he would never hesitate to use them, however. A professor of constitutional law and a staunch proponent of the adversary system of justice, he didn't concern himself with guilt or innocence, except as a jury might so find. I once asked if he would have any trouble going full bore for an acquittal for mass murderer Ted Bundy. He said no.

According to the legal system, that's how Lemann should feel. As a cop and citizen, Bundy and others of his mold (i.e., those who will almost surely kill again) make me wonder just how far and to what extent a lawyer should go. These considerations didn't trouble Buddy Lemann, and I suppose, in my heart of hearts, he was the kind of lawyer I would want representing me.

Some cops, having heard themselves described as a torturer torn from the pages of the Spanish Inquisition, would have confronted Mr. Lemann outside the courtroom. After all, this is public record, and the press reprints these charges—as the *Times-Picayune* did in this instance, making it tough on the detectives' kids at school. But those cops would have made a mistake; Buddy was just doing his job. Policemen who have been around are supposed to recognize this and harbor no hard feelings. It's all sort of an inside joke among judges, prosecutors, defense lawyers, detectives: a kind of big happy club. But the jury is never part of it, nor the people who read newspapers, and I didn't like it.

Buddy Lemann stopped me in the corridor after the preliminary hearing. He wanted to complain about his bad luck in drawing Judge Matthew Braniff. "With that guy," Buddy said, "there's no need for a prosecutor."

I didn't say anything. After all, Lemann and I stood on opposite sides of the fence. I did know that Judge Braniff was a decorated World War II gunner pilot who volunteered with and fought for the RAF *before* America even entered the fight, and he had always seemed fair to me.

"We'll win regardless," Buddy told me, smiling wickedly, rising up on his toes like a bantam rooster. "The prosecution's only got one thing going for it."

On the contrary, I thought we had everything. But I couldn't resist, so I asked, "What one thing, Buddy?"

"Why, you, John," he said through an impish grin. "You're the one thing. I never take you lightly."

He turned and marched down the corridor, followed by his retinue of adoring students, leaving me to worry, as I'm sure he intended, about exactly what he meant.

# •15•

ALTON Tumblin's girlfriend, Diane Hayes, heard it all. Unfortunately, she was taking a bath and didn't *see* anything.

Diane heard the doorbell ring just after 8:00 P.M. on September 2, 1978. She heard Alton answer it. She heard three shots ring out.

Our star witness was struck three times by bullets from a .38 handgun: in the right shoulder, abdomen, and head. He died instantly. Homicide Detectives John Norwood and Frank McNeil, on the scene within fifteen minutes, found Tumblin sprawled on the porch of his residence at 2510 Dumaine Street.

I found out about the murder when I reported for graveyard, and followed the investigation closely over the days, weeks, and months to come. Norwood and McNeil did everything humanly possible to track down the killer, but they had no murder weapon, no witness, and only one motive, which couldn't be proved or disproved because Harold Patin remained at large. Candy himself was in jail awaiting a trial already twice postponed.

I had liked "Red" Tumblin and brooded for a long time

that perhaps I should have done more to protect him. Just like Sheppard's death, I thought it a terrible waste, a terrible tragedy. I had told Tumblin to be careful, to call me if he felt the slightest danger, but clearly these warnings had been inadequate. He would have objected strenuously to protective custody, and I'm not sure we could have enforced it: He hadn't witnessed the murder of Sheppard, merely provided, unwittingly, the vehicle that transported the body to Almonaster.

Was that why he died?

Cynthia McCants, Patin's girlfriend, had warned Tumblin not to tell the police about Patin borrowing the car. Norwood and McNeil questioned Cynthia at length, but she denied any knowledge of Alton Tumblin's murder.

The trickle of little things going wrong had turned into a Niagara of negatives. Tumblin had been very important to the John Smith prosecution, providing a key missing link—how Sheppard's body got from the Marais Street apartment to the Almonaster swamp. Now, despite having Tumblin's signed and sworn statement, the evidence could not be used at trial. Joe Meyer would not be allowed to mention the borrowed car in court because the defense could not cross-examine, would be denied the constitutional right of confronting a witness against the accused.

Joe Meyer grimaced whenever he thought about our lost witness, but the next bizarre turn of events provoked the prosecutor to pounding his fist on his desk and a string of choice expletives. The McKnights, the couple who took over the Marais Street apartment after Candy and who would testify that the blood was there when they'd moved in, had packed up and vacated the premises, leaving no forwarding address. Normally this would have been a minor annoyance—we'd simply track them down—but

Curtis and Karen McKnight became as elusive as Harold Patin's and Sheppard's blood types.

I thought that to an outsider we must look like a detective version of the Keystone Kops. We lost Alton Tumblin. We couldn't locate Patin. We couldn't find the McKnights. We couldn't type Sheppard's blood. In pursuit of the latter, Dick Price had even enlisted contacts of his in the CIA, for heaven's sake, and to no avail.

"Candy," Joe Meyer told me one afternoon in his office, "has been the luckiest guy in the world. He drew Buddy Lemann and that pack of law school students out of a hat, and that's just the start."

A big start, I thought. Any ordinary public defender would already have tried to plea-bargain, or at least started the process. Lemann continued to act as if he held all the cards. It demonstrated once again to me what a crapshoot the system we call criminal justice really is. The difference between death in the electric chair and walking out of court a free man *might* come down to which lawyer stood next in line to represent an indigent defendant. This case also emphasized that all the evidence in the world is useless if a jury isn't allowed to hear it. The people judging Candy Smith would never know about Alton Tumblin, or the McKnights (unless we found them), even though we had their statements. I could hear in my mind Buddy Lemann emphasizing to the jury that the blood at Marais Street might have come from someone *the McKnights* murdered.

"We've got Candy's confession," I said to Joe Meyer that afternoon in his office. I wasn't trying to pump optimism into this star prosecutor. The confession really was enough, I believed. Jurors could not only read what John Smith said, they could hear him say it on tape.

"Yeah," Meyer agreed. He looked tired to me. He had

been pushing himself and his investigators hard, and we hadn't even gone to trial yet.

*"In his own words,"* I said, "Candy revealing a dozen details he couldn't have known if he hadn't been there. We know he's guilty, to a dead certainty. A jury will know."

"Maybe."

"What do you mean, maybe?"

"John, *we* don't believe that confession. I know it shouldn't make any difference. A murder was committed during the commission of a felony, which makes Smith as guilty as those who tugged on the electrical cord, but . . ."

"*He* tugged on the electrical cord. He . . ."

"Listen to me! We believe that. All right, we *know* it. But that's not how the confession plays. What Smith said makes him guilty, but Lemann is going to call thunder down from the sky to prove that we don't really believe our own confession. And that's true enough. We can only hope that when Buddy gets through obfuscating, the jurors will be intelligent enough to see what we realize had to have happened."

Jury selection began February 6, 1979, more than a year after Mark Sheppard's death. In what should have been a routine procedure, once again one of the "little things" cropped up and made me wonder if bringing John Smith to justice had been hopelessly jinxed.

It was a terrible day outside—cold, windy, stormy—and Senior Criminal District Court Judge Bernard Bagert ordered the jury pool commissioner not to bring in any jurors because of the inclement weather. This pronouncement was duly reported on radio and TV but misunderstood by Judge Matthew Braniff, who thought the order had been issued by the press. Braniff rescinded Judge Bagert's order, saying, "I run this court, not the news media."

It took ten hours to select the jury, a very long time by

New Orleans standards. Buddy Lemann, aiming to pick what he called a "unique" panel, was responsible for most of the delay. In brainstorming sessions with his students, the defense attorney decided to aim for what he called "a jury of Archie Bunkers." Usually, in a murder trial the accused's lawyer will move heaven and earth to find liberals, blacks, and other minorities, people widely believed less sympathetic to the testimony of police, less impressed by the righteousness of the state, more apt to relate to the disadvantaged background of the defendant.

Lemann turned all this reasoning around. He intended to make Mark Sheppard the defendant and Candy Smith the victim. Quite simply, he believed the Bunkers of the world—when put to the test—would dislike gays more than blacks. It would be a veiled "Sheppard-got-what-was-coming-to-him" defense, which Buddy didn't for a moment believe, but was perfectly in tune with doing what it takes to win.

During voir dire, Lemann let potential jurors know what he intended to prove. "I agree with the district attorney," he said, "that the evidence will show Doctor Sheppard was homosexual, but I disagree that my client, John Smith, is homosexual. In street terminology he is what is called 'straight.' Nevertheless, the evidence will show he sold his body, quite bluntly, to Doctor Mark Sheppard so the doctor could perform homosexual acts on him."

Translation: Straight is better than gay, Candy isn't one of "them."

Joe Meyer didn't care what tactics Buddy Lemann employed in jury selection. He had the confession to play to the jury, powerful proof of Smith's guilt, and plenty of corroborative evidence from the mouth of the defendant himself.

Meyer didn't object to seating Bunker types, and most of the more than one hundred rejected jurors were excused because they expressed reservations about the death penalty. It was remarkable, watching the two lawyers in action. Prosecutor Meyer found himself out of character seeking more moderate types. When the jury had finally been seated, Lemann judged he had six of "my people."

Darkness descended before I left Judge Braniff's court for the drive home to Slidell, and on the road I thought hard about the case for what seemed the thousandth time. I believed it brought into clear focus many of the aspects of criminal justice that troubled me most: The effort to imply, predominantly in rape cases, that the victim got what she deserved; preventing the prosecution from mentioning a defendant's prior record (if he has none, the defense can introduce this information by calling character witnesses); rules of evidence precluding the jury from reading statements, such as those made by the slain Alton Tumblin—in this case, like Mafia hit trials, it could pay to murder witnesses; and rules of evidence forbidding the prosecution from explaining its actions, i.e., why Wendell Blanks wasn't on trial.

Lemann made a big commotion about the absence of Wendell Blanks. Smith, after all, had named his former roommate as one of the killers. We didn't believe Blanks was guilty, but were not allowed to say why.

The normally reserved *Times-Picayune* headline "Murder Trial Will Be Lurid" over reporter Russell Goodman's byline gave the following account of the first day's action in the *State of Louisiana vs. John Edward Smith:*

> "This story is going to have a lurid aspect, an aspect we cannot deny. The doctor was a homosexual and part of his reasons for coming to New Orleans was to seek homosexual activity."

That was part of the prosecutor's opening remarks Wednesday to the jurors in the trial of John Edward "Candy" Smith, the man accused of the first-degree strangulation murder last Jan. 20 of St. Petersburg doctor Mark Sheppard.

The two main characters in Assistant District Attorney Joe Meyer's "story" include the Florida anesthesiologist and art collector, who is alleged to have walked a tenuous line, leading a straight life in the prominent circles in which he moved in his home town and traveling to New Orleans to solicit sex from young black men. The other character is the defendant, 21-year-old Smith, portrayed by defense counsel Arthur Lemann III as an uneducated, poor street hustler who made his living off pool games, dice and cards, and prostituting his body.

However, Lemann's version of the "story" is summed up by his opening remarks to the jury Wednesday. "This is a trial about two men who liked each other. One of those men is unfortunately dead. The state is now asking you to kill the other man." Lemann characterized the relationship of Smith and Dr. Sheppard as one which had turned from purely sexual to mutual respect and friendship.

Lemann told the jury Dr. Sheppard was a man who enjoyed picking up strange men for purposes of oral sex, enjoying the flirtation with the danger of such encounters. The prosecutor acknowledged the victim courted peril and paid for it with his life Jan. 20, 1978, when he was ambushed by Smith and two of the defendant's hard-luck friends as the doctor arrived at Smith's apartment to keep a prior date. No one else has been charged in the case by police.

Reporters flown in by Florida newspapers, some of Sheppard's friends from the Tampa Bay area, plus the usual gathering of murder-trial buffs from New Orleans itself, increased the big crowd that heard the opening day of testimony. A cross section of the legal community—receptionists, paralegals, trial lawyers, judges—took early or late lunches and breaks between court sessions to pop in and catch snatches of the battle between the star prosecutor and the ace defense lawyer. Of course, there were all those law school students, two of whom sat at the defense table with Lemann and actually conducted some of the questioning.

For jurisprudence aficionados this law arena provided the same charged atmosphere that revs up sports fans at a World Series game or a Super Bowl. They came to watch a headline case with a prominent victim and two heavyweight lawyers banging heads.

Dr. Paul McGarry from the coroner's office testified that animals and insects had stripped the flesh off Sheppard's right arm. The pathologist's clinical description of the badly decomposed face—lips and nose eaten away by maggots—gave listeners only an inkling of the stomach-turning sight we had encountered on Almonaster. He explained how positive identification had been possible by matching the doctor's teeth to his dental charts.

McGarry confirmed that the cause of death was strangulation. He could not verify that death would have taken five or six minutes. But Joe Meyer hinted it had—as the court would hear later from Smith's own lips—and he indicated those sitting in judgment should consider how long, how merciless, and how painful that time must have seemed to the victim.

Ursulines Guest House manager Jim Owens stated that the last time he had seen Dr. Sheppard was about 7:30 A.M. on January 20. Owens confirmed earlier testimony from Big Hector that there had been no apparent struggle in Sheppard's room.

Buddy Lemann didn't dwell on the anatomical facts Dr.

McGarry reported. But from the guest house manager—who fit right into the defense attorney's plan to try Mark Sheppard—he elicited testimony concerning the Floridian's sexual propensities. Owens stated: "In the most succinct term, Doctor Sheppard was his (Smith's) sugar daddy. I remember he gave me an envelope once for Candy which I assumed had a check in it." Meyer objected to this "assumption" and Braniff instructed the jury to ignore it. "He told me one of the reasons he liked the guest house was because he could lessen the risk of bringing young men back there instead of going to their houses. He said he liked oral sex with muscular, well-endowed black males who only wanted money from him."

I followed Owens on the stand, and Joe Meyer led me through the entire complex investigation, including the recording of John Smith's confession. After so many appearances in other murder trials, I knew, like Joe Friday, to stick only to the facts. In my head were images of *five minutes* of intense pain and suffering, and the indifference of those who were the killers, but all I could do was relate what I knew and hope it moved the jury.

It didn't move Buddy Lemann. Showing little interest in *what* Smith confessed—that a man had been savagely murdered in his apartment—the lawyer made much ado about *why* his client had given the statement.

LEMANN: You beat those statements out of John Smith, didn't you, Detective Dillmann?

DILLMANN: No, sir.

LEMANN: You smashed his feet with a blackjack, didn't you?

DILLMANN: No, sir.

LEMANN: You also used that blackjack on his testicles, didn't you?

DILLMANN: I did not. I didn't have a blackjack.

LEMANN: You used your knee, perhaps?
DILLMANN: I didn't touch him. Neither did Steve London.
LEMANN: You stood over Mr. Smith, didn't you, and pulled hairs out of his face?
DILLMANN: I did not.

And so it went. Any judge on the planet who believed Lemann's charges would have called for an immediate investigation of police brutality, but, of course, none was forthcoming. These accusations were so commonplace, so much a part of the "game," that none of the inner circle took them seriously. But what about the jury? What about people reading tomorrow morning's newspaper? What about—no, I could rely on them—*my family?*

Lemann attacked my testimony by innuendo. Too shrewd to drag out a frontal assault on a peace officer, the crafty public defender kept referring to me as "smooth and cool John Dillmann," and hoped his sarcastic overtones would transmit a different signal to his listeners: "Distinguished members of the jury, before you sits a barbaric pig who stooped to beating and coercing a confession from my frightened client. Don't for a moment let yourselves be fooled by this monster whose bestial dark half feeds on intimidation and power plays." If Lemann could have read my mind, he would have known my thoughts *about him* and the attempted character assassination were neither smooth nor cool. But I had to maintain my composure and give the jury credit for being able to see through this charade.

My appearance on the stand afforded Lemann another opportunity to vilify Mark Sheppard, and he took full advantage. He dug out every detail I knew about Sheppard's secret, tawdry life-style in New Orleans, no doubt hoping to fuel any prejudices jurors had that somehow the anesthesiologist got what he deserved.

* * *

The third day of the trial, Thursday, February 8, 1979, was largely devoted to the playing of John Smith's tape-recorded confession, which jurors followed on neatly typed transcripts. The veniremen listened intently, often checking voice against words on the pages. They had sworn to do their duty, not a particularly difficult job, I thought, in view of what they heard and read in black and white.

Buddy Lemann projected monumental unconcern during the several hours the tape droned on. His attitude: Why bother listening to this fantastic tale that was beaten out of my client by savage policemen? At the confession's conclusion, Smith conceded he had not been abused, but somehow to Lemann this was proof that he had.

The prosecution rested its case.

Lemann called Daisy Scott posthaste to rebuff the just-played eyewitness account of the murder, to in essence push the erase button before the "coerced" tape-recorded statement had time to sink into the minds of the jurors. Here is the *Times-Picayune*'s accurate report of Daisy Scott's testimony:

> She claimed she and Smith had lived together for a couple of years, though they often had different apartments. She told the jurors before Criminal District Court Judge Matthew Braniff that Smith was in her company most of Jan. 20. He left her apartment at 1451 St. Claude that morning about 8 A.M. but returned an hour later, she said. They left together at noon that day, but then Smith left her downtown so he could "hustle some money." She explained that meant to play pool and cards or to shoot dice on the corner. "Hustle his body, too?" Lemann asked her. "I don't know anything about that," she replied, though she said Smith informed her of his relationship with the

> physician. She told the attorney Smith spent the night with her Jan. 20 in her apartment.

An angry Joe Meyer challenged Daisy Scott: "Name one single person who saw you and Candy together on January 20."

"I can't," she said. "That happened too long ago for me to remember."

Next came the moment for which everyone had waited. Buddy Lemann called John Smith to the witness box. Candy looked sharp in a blue suit, complementary tie, starched white shirt, and spit-shined shoes.

Lemann had so far done everything he could. A latecomer to the trial might have thought someone named Mark Sheppard stood in the dock. But now the defense lawyer needed help, and the defendant would have to do his part to save his own hide. There was no way to win without putting Candy on the stand.

Smith glanced at the jurors, probably following the advice of those law students who had instructed him on the importance of eye contact, but then he quickly looked away, not what his mentors wanted.

Buddy Lemann, oozing courtesy and concern, conducted the questioning: "John," he asked, "do you understand the seriousness of the offense the jury heard you confessing to during that taped statement?"

"Yeah," Candy answered. I guessed his diction coaches groaned inwardly. "I heard what I was led into saying."

"What do you mean, John, 'led into saying'?"

"Dillmann told me beforehand what he wanted to hear."

"Why did you go along with it?"

"Out of fear. They beat on me repeatedly. I just followed Dillmann's lead on all the questions. I felt like I would say anything that came to mind—anything I thought Dillmann wanted to hear."

"The men beating you, those were Detectives Steve London and John Dillmann?"

"Yeah."

"Tell the jury, John, exactly what they did."

"They pulled hair from my chin. Just yanked it right out. They hit my feet and punched me in my privates with something that looked like a blackjack."

"And these beatings are why you made this confession, correct?"

"Yeah. I took a gamble when I made that statement so that I wouldn't get beat up anymore. I'm a gambler. I was gambling that I could prove my innocence later. I figured they'd find Red and Harold, both of them would have alibis, and then everybody would know I'd made this all up."

Smith, during the confession, had offered a different reason for coming clean:

DILLMANN: John, why have you made this statement? For what reason?

SMITH: I guess my conscience.

DILLMANN: Has it bothered you, John?

SMITH: It has. My old lady could tell something was bothering me, but she ain't never know what it was.

When Lemann finished, Meyer tore into Candy like a tiger. How did he know about the yellow bedsheet? About the sock in Dr. Sheppard's mouth? The electrical cord pulled from the radio?

His knowledge of the radio was crucial. *I* hadn't known the cord had come from a radio *until* Smith made his confession. How could I possibly have coaxed that response out of him in the interrogation room?

Meyer radiated scorn for Candy. He asked, rhetorically, why, if London and I had terrorized Smith so completely, we hadn't gone one extra step and put the murder weapon in his hands.

Smith sweated a lot, stammered, hedged, bent, but never broke. Under any pressure, his coaches had told him, stick to your guns.

And he did. There would be no Perry Mason-type witness-stand confession in this trial. No way would John Smith finally crack, admit his guilt, and throw himself on the mercy of the court. Candy, the self-professed gambler, stoically maintained his poker face to the end.

All that remained were the closing arguments and Judge Braniff's instructions to the jury. The four days of the trial—the first three had run into the night, as the judge attempted to slightly unclog a snarled court docket and wrap up the case before the weekend—had exhausted everyone, but the protaganist lawyers dug deep inside themselves in one last mighty effort to win.

Meyer spoke first, the logic of his argument as insistent as a jackhammer, though tempered with numerous allusions to Greek drama. The seven-man, five-woman jury consisted of several medical professionals, a retired university professor, an antique dealer, an engineer, and an architect. Calling Smith's claims "preposterous," referring often to the confession, leading the jury step by step through the events of January 20, Meyer summed it up in his final paragraph: "This is a case of high tragedy where we have a person with sterling qualities, but with one fatal flaw he cannot escape. I'm not suggesting that Doctor Sheppard's flaw was that he was homosexual, but that he was constantly seeking out danger, courting something other than sexual relationships—death. That courtship came to full bloom January 20, 1978, in that Marais Street apartment."

Buddy Lemann hopped to his feet the moment Meyer finished, declaring he wanted to waste no time on the "fantasies" of Meyer's argument. Buddy, the consummate showman, passionate and articulate, spoke in a hushed courtroom to an audience straining to hear. He had been described as "the master of the close," and he didn't disappoint. "Essentially what Mr. Meyer is asking is that you disbelieve his own evidence," Buddy said, his voice the soul of reason. " *'I hadn't committed no murder. I was just a witness.'* The state doesn't want you to believe that. *'I didn't know they were going to kill him, no. All I knew is I thought they were going to take his money.'* They don't want you to believe that!"

Lemann looked aggrieved, horrified. "They want you to go beyond the evidence, to *speculate* that John Smith killed the doctor."

Next he attacked me, "smooth and cool John Dillmann," who only revealed his sadism to innocent murder suspects.

"Why did Mr. Smith implicate himself by making a statement?" Lemann asked the jurors. He knew he had to overcome that confession. "The police told him, 'You knew the doctor, you've been to his Florida home, you've got blood on your walls.' John Smith says he's a gambler. He gave them stuff. He told them what they wanted to hear. They'll say his alibi is shoddy. Well, sure it's shoddy; my client is shoddy. Think about it. John Smith can't be expected to know exactly where he was the day Doctor Sheppard is presumed to have been strangled with the radio cord because Smith didn't lead the life of a professional recorded on a desk calendar."

Lemann professed profound understanding of "Smith's unfortunate life of hustling from pool tables to corner dice games to peddling his body, living in a world of illiterates and only knowing associates through the veil of nicknames. This man is supposed to have a trial by his peers, but none of you in your sophisticated life-styles can be considered his peer."

It seemed to me Buddy was trying to square a circle, and

I feared he might succeed. "You solid citizens," he said to the jury, "would never consider making a false statement like this to the police. But John Smith is afraid of the police. You need to understand that his fear caused him to make statements that none of you would ever consider."

Buddy was far from finished. Although he knew the answers perfectly well, he pounded the jury with questions that could cause them reasonable doubt. He asked again, why isn't Wendell Blanks on trial? Where is Harold Patin? How do you know the McKnights didn't kill someone in that apartment? Where *are* the McKnights?

Candy had testified that he didn't know how to operate an automobile and never had a driver's license. That being the case, Buddy asked: "Ladies and gentlemen, how could Mr. Smith have driven the body out to Almonaster Avenue?"

A nice diversion, I thought, one the jury might not catch. I wanted to stand up with an interruption and remind them that we never said Candy was behind the wheel. In fact, he had stated quite clearly in the confession that Patin drove.

Lemann threw out many lines, brilliantly, hoping the jury would latch onto at least one. It seemed to me he turned the law upside down when he claimed Smith couldn't be convicted of felony murder because only forty dollars had been stolen. True, a felony required theft of one hundred dollars or more, but we only had Smith's word for the amount taken. Also, Buddy said, a toy gun (which Smith claimed was used—again, we had only his word on it) meant no armed robbery had taken place. Even, God forbid, if you believe the confession, he said, you can't convict because no felony was intended.

Hogwash. What could any reasonable person think Candy Smith *intended* when he agreed to allow Dr. Sheppard to be robbed in his own apartment? That Sheppard wouldn't go to the police? That the doctor would permit himself to be roughed up, strangled, and say nothing about it?

Buddy had an answer for this, too: Sheppard would have kept his mouth shut because reporting the incident would have damaged his reputation and, besides, why would Candy "kill the goose that laid the golden eggs? A prostitute doesn't kill his Number-One john."

Well, this one did, and Meyer had presented testimony from a habitué of Cigar's that John Smith had learned, prior to the murder, about Sheppard giving that expensive cue stick to Ponce Woods, and also about the dinner date with Larry Cephas. John Smith had been "very angry, very jealous." Maybe he figured the goose was headed elsewhere.

Buddy Lemann was something to see. The man who later got Carlos Marcello out of prison was at his prime-time best, one moment eliciting sympathy for his client's sad background, the next evoking rage over police brutality, and finally raising the specter of a railroaded black defendant being wrongfully hurried along to his execution to avenge the murder of a rich, prominent white doctor. And always, sometimes hidden, sometimes not, the "H" word.

With the intensity of a great conductor having brought his orchestra to the crashing crescendo, Buddy thundered out his dramatic conclusion: "We've reached the day of judgment, the moment of judgment. This case is not about high tragedy and low tragedy. It's about *one great tragedy,* and whether or not it's compounded is in your hands."

It would almost be unfortunate, I thought, for him to lose this case, after giving such a virtuoso performance. But only "almost." Substance counted more than form, and laws that judged murder the most serious of crimes took precedence over the good show Buddy had put on.

But something more. Lemann's main hope of winning, it seemed to me, involved the jury somehow deciding that Sheppard's sexual preference made him a legitimate target for killers. If such a notion ever took hold, I feared, no one different from the norm could ever feel safe. And what would be the norm?

Joe Meyer owned the last chance to address the jury. With everyone now completely worn out, this special prosecutor concentrated, almost like an elementary school teacher reemphasizing basic principles of arithmetic, on the inescapable logic of the state's case.

The jury retired at 4:00 P.M. to deliberate. We hoped for a quick verdict, which usually meant guilty. The longer deliberations dragged on, according to courtroom wisdom, the greater the likelihood of a hung jury or acquittal. I had seen juries convict in five minutes, sending a resounding vote of approval to the prosecution, but knew it wouldn't happen here. Lemann's razzle-dazzle, now-there's-evidence, now-there-isn't defense would require time to wade through.

I called Diane, grabbed a sandwich, and went back to Headquarters. I was just beginning to tackle my logjam of paperwork when the phone rang.

"The jury's coming in," Joe Meyer told me.

I glanced at my watch, at first disbelieving, and then I felt a surge of elation: 7:10 P.M. They had been out only three hours, ten minutes, a winning time for the people of Louisiana.

When I met Joe Meyer in the corridor outside Judge Braniff's courtroom, we agreed it had taken a superior jury to cut through Buddy Lemann's self-generated fog.

I caught a glimpse of Buddy bouncing into the courtroom, accompanied by his entourage. "Never let them see you sweat" was the theme of a 1980s deodorant commercial, but Lemann practiced that dictum long before the ad. His face was unreadable, but I believed he had to know: Quick verdict meant guilty.

But it didn't. The jury foreman announced that his panel stood "hopelessly deadlocked," those causing "the impasse numbered substantially more than one," and "nothing could be resolved by further deliberations."

I expected Judge Braniff to send them back with a stern warning to try harder, if necessary for several days, even a week. Instead he thanked the jurors and dismissed them.

Meyer struck his fist hard on the prosecution table; I stared into space, numb.

Practically anywhere else in the country that jury would have been ordered to deliberate further, but in New Orleans, for reasons I never adequately understood, a judge usually accepted the jury's word about being deadlocked.

I believe that inwardly Buddy Lemann was elated, but he displayed a demeanor of disappointment and even shock over the jury not setting his client free. However, his mood probably was genuinely deflated when he learned the jury had deadlocked at 6-6, with the half dozen who wanted to convict consisting entirely of those he had labeled as Archie Bunkers.

Had Lemann gotten the jury he wanted, Candy Smith would have been on his way to the electric chair.

Reporters trailed a hurrying Joe Meyer down the corridor. "Will there be another trial?" one of them asked.

"Definitely," Meyer shouted over his shoulder. "We're very disappointed. Of course Smith will be tried again."

# • 16 •

BEAT patrolman Steve Reboul churned his legs furiously—up and down, up and down—straining every muscle to shorten the two-stride advantage maintained by the fugitive ahead of him, running as though his life depended on escape. Led on a steeplechase over obstacles draped in darkness, Reboul sidestepped lawn sprinklers and garden hoses stretched across several yards, dodged garbage cans and shadowy mirages down an alley, and darted between parked cars on a side street. Only three yards separated leader from trailer. The one in back, the good guy, resembled a water skier being pulled along by a tow rope—the bad guy's lead never varied. The athletic Reboul believed it might come down to an endurance test and didn't relish being marathon man.

It was 10:00 P.M. in New Orleans on this humid, steamy May 2, 1979. I know how this cop in a footrace must have felt: out of breath, heart pounding, salty sweat pouring like acid into burning eyes, wondering why the hell not just let him go? Catching him meant a struggle, a fight, perhaps personal injury. The fleeing figure wouldn't go peacefully; he'd already proven that.

Reboul and his partner Paul Blocksom had responded to a domestic disturbance report from a neighbor complaining about a loud fight at 619 North Miro Street. When the door opened, a black man looked from one cop to the other, then without warning plowed his fist into Blocksom's face, charged through the open door, shouldering Reboul off balance, and started to run.

"Police! Halt!" Reboul shouted several times as their feet pounded out a syncopated cadence of constant rhythm on grass, ground, and gravel. The patrolman soon abandoned his ploy of issuing verbal commands that only drained needed wind. The guy obviously wasn't going to stop. If Reboul could just maintain touch—he was sure Blocksom had radioed for help—he could soon learn why this man had risked assaulting two police officers instead of answering their questions. Having responded to a routine call, they would be surprised to find out the runaway had bolted to avoid a possible murder charge.

But Reboul knew he couldn't maintain touch for long. The object of his chase was going to pull away at any moment, and the cop summoned every spiritual and physical resource at his disposal for one last heart-bursting spurt and dive. With a flying shoestring tackle he sent the fugitive tumbling to the sidewalk.

They rolled on the ground, clawing, kicking, punching, but Reboul finally won when he pinned the suspect face-down on the pavement and cuffed his hands behind him.

We never learned how often Harold Patin visited his girlfriend Cynthia McCants at her North Miro Street address. She said this was the first time; he said nothing. From this man who would make the sphinx sound chatty came the only words he *ever* spoke to us: "I want to see my lawyer."

That was that. The hard-eyed, stone-faced ex-con didn't have to wait for a Miranda reading to assert his rights. He came out with his declaration before Blocksom and Reboul even got him to Central Lockup.

That's where I had my first look at him. A real tough with an I've-been-through-this-routine-before demeanor, Patin met my gaze with a steady, confident stare. I suspected nothing could ever crack it, not even his own conviction for murder, should our plan work out: Convict Candy, then turn the male prostitute into a star witness against the individual we suspected was his partner.

Actually, I didn't think "partner" was the right description. I had John Smith pegged as a moral vacuum, able to commit a murder without qualm or a look back, but for me *active evil* seeped from the persona of Harold Patin. If the tragedy that befell Dr. Sheppard had required a driving, malignant source, it was this man, boring his cold, challenging eyes into mine through the bars of his cell.

John Smith's retrial began Thursday, June 6, 1979—D day we called it. The crowd in Judge Braniff's courtroom was smaller—less interest on a second go-round—and except for one new player, Harold Patin, the drama basically had the same actors and script.

This time Buddy Lemann sought out a more conventional defense-oriented jury, welcoming blacks, minorities, and white liberals, people who he thought would be more receptive to charges of police brutality and sympathize with John Smith's background. He had to persuade them—this was the key—that Smith came from a different world, one which made the defendant's "false" confession not just understandable but virtually inevitable.

Joe Meyer said he searched for intelligence, nothing more, in the jurors. They needed to see through Lemann's theatrics and charisma to the heart of what happened, what *had* to have occurred in light of that confession and all the corroboration it contained.

Buddy early on called Patin to the stand. The witness might have been a young, rising executive, if judged from the clothes Lemann provided him, fancy duds that didn't camouflage his cold, hard vibe. I thought his claims of knowing nothing about the Sheppard murder rang untrue.

The appearance of Harold Patin allowed Joe Meyer to enter into the trial record that Alton Tumblin, the man who said he loaned his car to Patin, was not present at the trial because he had been murdered. In chambers Judge Braniff had admonished Meyer not to make the slightest inference in court that Patin had an excellent motive for Tumblin's murder, so the prosecutor could go no further than dangle the fact of the death in the air.

Patin had been charged with first-degree murder right after his arrest, but we hadn't brought the matter to the grand jury yet. We probably never would if Smith got acquitted, which made the pressure to win this case terrific. Even though this trial was to decide the guilt or innocence of John "Candy" Smith, the fate of Patin also hung in the balance.

Dr. Paul McGarry again testified. So did Larry Cephas. George Heath. Jim Owens.

When landlord Roland Gee was questioned, he stated his cleanup crew had not reported finding any blood as they prepared the apartment for new tenants. Well, we didn't think this "cleanup crew," two part-timers, had given Candy's old place the white glove treatment expected from maids at some place like the Ritz or the Fairmont Hotel. The bulk of the blood deposits had been out of plain view, sandwiched between the baseboards and flooring, and the spatters on the wall could have been mistaken for any number of stains by someone unaccustomed to the sight of dried blood.

Regardless, Buddy Lemann's allusions to the McKnights

increased and grew darker. Why weren't the police looking for this sinister couple?

We were, but not as murder suspects. And Meyer's investigators continued the search for a source of Sheppard's blood type, while Homicide Detectives Norwood and McNeil accelerated their quest for clues to Alton Tumblin's execution-style murder.

Neither of the attorneys had an easy job. They both had been on the case more than a year; and since the hung jury, each had spent the last four months looking for the break that would tilt the stalemate his way. It seemed to me we had the better shot. If we found the McKnights, or Sheppard's blood type, we believed Buddy Lemann would switch his class's focus from how to win a case to how to plea-bargain.

The second trial turned out to be just as heated as the first, but more interesting and with more finesse—if viewed as a chess match—each lawyer having had the opportunity to study the other's strategy and refine his own countermoves. Whenever it looked like the defense might be trying to put Mark Sheppard on trial again, Joe Meyer brought attention *back to the crime.* Lemann found sinister motives lurking everywhere, indicating we knew the blood type of Sheppard and refused to reveal it because the information would torpedo our case.

The truth was Lemann himself had his whole law class also searching for that blood type, and used his clinic's fund to hire a private investigator for the hunt. If it didn't match the samples from Candy's apartment, he could be counted on to burst into court with arms waving. If it did, he had no obligation to help the prosecution. But Lemann's legions were no more successful than ours.

Four additional months of coaching made Candy Smith a smoother witness during his second trial. He doubled over in a display of pain when miming that blackjack-to-the-testicles blow, and acted out believable visual histrionics and flinches when he described hair being torn from his face. "I couldn't take no more," he said. "I decided to gamble and tell 'em what they wanted to hear. That's what I did, and I figured they'd know I lied when they talked to Harold and Red."

"How could they coach you on that radio?" Meyer asked in cross-examination.

"Huh?"

"The radio. All they had was a cord from a small appliance that was used to strangle the doctor. *Before* your statement, they didn't know it had come from a radio, which they didn't find until the next day. They learned about its existence *from you.*"

"They must have already known. They told me what to say."

Meyer threw out a question to the jury: "Why do you think they didn't just kick the crap out of him and make him say *he* did it, instead of two other guys?"

Of course, Meyer had those Hollywood Walk television pictures, and the testimony of the assistant coroner, Monroe Samuels, and the admitting officer at Central Lockup, to aver that Smith had *not* been beaten. He also had the record, stamped with exact times and dates—that I carefully established—when we started the surveillance at Daisy Scott's residence, when we arrested the defendant, when we brought him to Headquarters, when we questioned him, and when we took him for a physical exam. There simply was no time in this logged sequence of events to coach Candy, much less beat him.

Buddy Lemann scoffed at all this. The police, the assistant coroner, the jailer, all might be part of a conspiracy, "a normal enough arrangement for people who work together."

I felt good and bad. Good because I had taken such care

to conduct myself just so, doing everything according to the book, including those four Miranda warnings. Bad because it seemed to me no matter how conscientiously an officer performed, he still ended up being portrayed to the jury and the public as a monster.

The closing arguments again were the climax of the trial. Meyer was effective as always, and Buddy Lemann a genuine spellbinder. Friends and associates had long been urging the public defender to have some of his best summations printed and bound, possibly as a textbook; his closes were that good.

The *Times-Picayune* story the next day continued the frustrating refrain:

> THIRD TRIAL AHEAD
> FOR MURDER SUSPECT
>
> John Edward "Candy" Smith will stand trial a third time for the first-degree murder of St. Petersburg physician Mark Sheppard, a prosecutor said Friday after jurors informed the court they were at a stalemate and could not reach a verdict.
>
> The action was the second time a jury before Criminal District Court Judge Matthew Braniff deadlocked in the trial and means the defendant will be remanded to Orleans Parish Prison where he has been confined since March 9, 1978, the day of his arrest.
>
> The jury of 12 deliberated 10½ hours over Thursday and Friday before the mistrial was declared. The exhausted defense attorney, Arthur Lemann III, thanked the jurors as they filed out. Prosecutors Joe Meyer Jr. and Conn Regan said the 22-year-old defendant definitely will face a third court date. Meyer summed up his exasperation succinctly: "Nuts."

This time the veniremen deadlocked 8-4, for acquittal, not an encouraging sign. Noting this, Judge Braniff granted bail for Smith, and we released Harold Patin. If we won the third trial, and Candy turned, as he surely would, we intended to indict Patin.

*Times-Picayune* reporter Russell Goodman wrote about an "exhausted" Buddy Lemann, and he was right on the mark. But it wasn't just Buddy. Joe Meyer had also reached the end of his rope, and neither lawyer wanted to go at it a third time. Buddy joked about "handling the same case for the rest of my life," unlikely because another hung jury would surely prompt Judge Braniff to dismiss the charges.

Just a few days after the second deadlock, Meyer announced a reduction of the charge to second degree. This meant Smith no longer faced the death penalty, a factor the prosecutor felt had contributed greatly to the jury's reluctance to convict. The second-degree murder charge required a 10-2 plurality, not the 12-0 needed for first degree.

But the problem, if it should be viewed as such, still might be the lawyers. Irresistible Force versus Immovable Object. Even 10-2 might prove beyond reach given the two closely matched attorneys and their undoubted ability to sway people.

Lemann and Meyer sat down to talk about the difficulty. Each indeed had consumed their fill of the Candy Smith case, and the time had come for them to work together and search out a way to resolve the matter. Lemann's solution involved dropping the charges: "You guys have already had two chances, and continuing with yet another trial will be unfair to the defendant." Meyer countered with a proposal that Candy plea-bargain: "We both know he's guilty, and this lucky streak he's riding is bound to end. You'll be doing him a favor."

Poles apart and given the egos involved, I wasn't surprised they remained at loggerheads. But these worn-out warriors did agree on one thing: They wanted out. Meyer and Lemann had "other things to do" besides try and defend John Smith in a case most people didn't care about any more. Forgotten was the big initial push from Chief Morris, the mobilization of the Homicide unit and the resultant massive investment of time and taxpayer's money, the fear of lost tourism and damaged reputations, and Dick Price making us look like a bunch of blundering buffoons. To some extent eighteen months and two hung juries had reduced the intense heat under the Mark Sheppard case to a slow simmer. The prevailing attitude was that we'd solved the case. Killers get caught in our town; what the courts do is not our business.

And surely this was a healthy way to look at the case. I knew it in my mind, but my heart said otherwise. I fed my ulcer by grousing about a judicial system whose rules made the dispensation of justice more dependent on the skills of competing lawyers than on a cool, rational analysis of the facts. What did it matter that Sheppard bought the services of young black prostitutes? Certainly that didn't give Candy Smith and Harold Patin the right to kill him, though surely Buddy's constant references to homosexuality (always pointing out in the next breath that Smith was straight) implied to the jury that *they* should consider the matter important.

"Dillmann, you're too involved," Dantagnan and Saladino counseled. Saladino, especially, seemed to have a handle on everything, and I had to admit he did practice what he preached: Do the absolute best you can, but separate yourself—you'll never be judge and jury, so have the wisdom to leave alone what you can't influence.

Usually I could, but it took work. Catching a murder suspect—especially in this case—often required a major expenditure of effort, and after pouring myself into it for so long and so completely I had trouble stamping CASE CLOSED on an investigation when my role ended. My total absorption and not being able to let go, making a clean break when a prosecutor took over a murder, caused me finally to let go of my career in Homicide. Six years down the line when I had to watch another guilty man—one we had sewn up forty ways to Sunday—beat a murder rap, I retired from NOPD. As in the John Smith case, I put everything I had into that later investigation, and though the logical part of my brain said accept the verdict and enjoy some peace of mind, I couldn't. I knew he was guilty.

Lemann and Meyer finally reached a compromise: They would both drop out of the case and leave the third trial to others. Many of Lemann's law school students were graduating, and there would be a new case for new pupils to start in the fall. And of course fresh challenges always awaited Joe Meyer, the DA's designated hitter for heaters. He turned the John Smith prosecution over to a young, newcomer named Bob Myers.

# • 17 •

I walked into Judge Braniff's courtroom on September 25, 1979, the morning Candy Smith's third trial began, and stopped dead in my tracks. Surely my eyes deceived me. I closed them, counted to three, looked again. There was Buddy Lemann shuffling papers at the defense table.

"I thought Lemann was out," I said to Bob Myers. "That deal he made with Joe . . ."

"Well, he's obviously not out. There he is."

"You mean?"

"He double-crossed us."

I caught Buddy's eye and he smiled at me. He appeared tanned and fit. A summer's rest had done him good. I knew right then that justice for Mark Sheppard was extremely unlikely. Young Myers had only three months of preparation—the brilliant Lemann already had two trials behind him—and even the DA's top gun hadn't been able to secure a conviction.

Joe Meyer had been snookered. Neither of us could do more than shrug dispiritedly and grudgingly acknowledge Buddy's chutzpah.

The case again came down to the closing arguments,

Lemann's forte. Twice his magical closes had resulted in hung juries. Miracles, I had thought, but this time he rose even above himself. His speech was so effective that it would have taken a rare jury to separate the bombast and misdirection from the hard facts that shouted "Guilty!" at Candy Smith. Buddy's close, better than anything else, explains Smith's fate, and for that reason alone deserves to be quoted completely and without interruption:

> May it please the court, members of the jury, I want to thank each of you for the great amount of time and attention you've given this case.
>
> What the district attorney says is correct. The only evidence they have in this case is the statement of Mr. Smith. When you cut through all the testimony—it's strange it took us four days to try this case—and when you get right down to it, there's only one piece of evidence, and that is the statement made by my client to Mr. Dillmann on March 9th. That's it.
>
> I want to examine with you that statement, and the law involved in this case. And I want to first of all approach it on the assumption that you believe every word of that statement of March 9th—believe every word of it.
>
> Now, the law of principals is not a very complicated principle of law. It's just common sense. It's partnership. That's all it means. Partners. If I pay a man to knock somebody off while I'm sitting in my law office not doing anything, I'm guilty. I wasn't there, but I'm guilty because I was a partner with this fellow.
>
> If two kids decide we're going to go into a store to shoplift, and one kid goes in and shoplifts while the other one stands outside as a lookout or a distraction, the kid outside is equally guilty. He's a partner. He's

equally guilty. But, the State must prove to you beyond a reasonable doubt that they were partners.

For example, if the two kids agree they are going into the store to shoplift, and they go into the store, and one kid all of a sudden pulls out a revolver and commits an armed robbery, the other kid is not guilty of armed robbery because it wasn't a partnership; he was not in partnership on that. He didn't agree to that. He's not guilty. If two people agree to shoplift, and one of them, on his own, decides to commit an armed robbery, the other person is not guilty of armed robbery because he didn't agree to it. He didn't know about it. That's an important principle that you have to apply in this case.

Let's take this statement, and let's assume you believe everything in the statement. What is Mr. Smith guilty of? He says in the statement that he agreed to allow Blanks and Patin to rip off the doctor. And, in the statement he says, "I didn't know anything about any armed robbery. I agreed to allow them to steal money." Now, that's stealing—theft is not armed robbery. In the classic sort of French Quarter prostitute situation, where the prostitute takes the customer up to her apartment and then an accomplice goes through the pants and steals the money, that's not armed robbery. That's not simple robbery. That's theft. So, if that is all the statement comes to, then Smith can't be found guilty of second-degree murder because throughout the statement he says, "I didn't know anything about any robbery. All I agreed to do was to let them rip off the doctor."

Now, the Judge will explain to you that there are three possible verdicts you can render in this case: second-degree murder, manslaughter, and not guilty. He will also instruct that it will take ten of you to reach any one of those verdicts. Ten of you at least must agree on any one of those three verdicts. If ten of you cannot reach an agreement, then a mistrial will be declared, and the State, if it so selects, can retry my client.

Let's consider manslaughter. His Honor will instruct on manslaughter. And, in manslaughter, it says, "A person may be guilty of manslaughter when a homicide is committed without any attempt to cause death or great bodily harm, when the offender is engaged in the perpetration or attempted perpetration of any felony not enumerated in the second-degree statute." However, theft is only a felony when the amount taken is more than a hundred dollars. And, in this case, if you believe that statement, the only thing taken was forty dollars.

I want to talk about this statement, and I want you to understand one thing, the most important thing, about this statement. I'm going to talk to you for a while because I know when I stop talking, I lose control of my client, and I've got to turn him over to you, and that frightens me. So I'm going to talk a lot.

If you carefully analyze the State's case, and if you carefully analyze the district attorney's argument to you and his persuasion and comments to you, it will come down to this: they, the State, do not believe this statement. They don't believe it. They don't believe it! And, that's the key to this whole case. They don't believe the statement.

I'm going to tell you what they don't believe. Page Three: "I never knew anything like this was going to take place until it happened. And, after it happened, it was too late for me to really do something. I hadn't did no crime. Well, I didn't think I had committed no crime. I hadn't murdered nobody. I mean, I was a witness." They don't believe that.

Page Sixteen: "Well, I didn't have no knowledge of

this armed robbery. All I know was they were going to take the money. I didn't know, you know, that there was going to be no armed robbery."

They don't believe that. And they don't want you to believe that.

"All right. Were you going to get any of the money from this robbery?" "All I was doing was letting them be in my apartment at that time. I have money, so I didn't need no money. I was just letting them make some money."

They don't believe that. And they don't want you to believe that part of the statement.

Page Seventeen: "I didn't know they was going to kill him, no. All I thought they was going to do is take his money. As far as the killing part, I didn't know this." They don't believe that.

I'll tell you something else. They don't believe this statement because you saw Mr. Patin. He was arrested, charged with the murder, interviewed by Dillmann. Dillmann checked it out and released him. Wendell Blanks, "Red," arrested by the police, interviewed by Dillmann, was released by Dillmann.

Now, don't let him tell you, or try to explain to you, because it's not evidence, why Patin and Blanks are not on trial. They have the same evidence against Patin and Blanks as they do against Smith. This statement, they could play this statement on that recorder, at a trial with Patin sitting there, or Wendell Blanks sitting there. You know why they don't do it? Because that's all they have, and they know it's a flimflam. It's a false statement. And they don't want you to believe this statement, when you get right down to it.

What they want you to do is to look at this statement and pick and choose. They want you to think, "Well, this part of it's got to be true, but this part of it isn't true." But, they don't give you any evidence to justify, no corroborative evidence whatsoever. None.

Motive is not an element of a crime, but motive is very important to common-sense people, because people in the ordinary course of life know that people have motives for doing things. Mr. Myers here first tries the motive of armed robbery. Well, he doesn't like that motive too much, because he can't deny the fact that John Smith could have gotten any amount of money at any time he wanted to from the doctor. Why in the world would John Smith want to rob the doctor? The doctor gave him anything he wanted. So, he kind of flirts with robbery for a little bit. Then, he says, well, we'll try something else: jealousy. That's his big motive, that John Smith, the whore, who sold his body, was jealous of another whore. If so, why was he jealous of Ponce Woods and not jealous of Larry Cephas? I don't really know. The most important question, if jealousy was the motive, is why would he kill the doctor and not Ponce Woods? When have you ever heard of a jealous whore killing her customer instead of the other whore that the customer has turned to? The doctor was the goose that laid the golden egg for John Smith. If another person was getting some of the golden eggs, what would you do? You don't kill the goose that lays the golden egg. You kill the other person who is running off with the golden eggs.

You don't have to take my word that they know it's a weak case. You heard it yourself at the beginning of the trial. The indictment, which was originally first degree, was amended to second degree because they recognize the weakness in their case.

You have to remember that whatever evidence we've

been able to gather shows that this statement really is false, and was just—well, Smith gave them something to give them something.

First of all, when the doctor was missing in January, Detective Heath went to the guest house. He was in charge then. And, at that time, all the New Orleans police had was a missing person. There are two very important things that happened. The doctor's wallet was there, and the credit cards were there.

When the doctor's body was found in February, a month later, then John Dillmann takes over the case. But he doesn't know that Heath, at the guest house, had seen the doctor's wallet, had seen the credit cards. But in this statement, John Smith said he took forty dollars from the doctor's wallet. *From the wallet.* How could this be possible? According to Detective Heath, the wallet was at the hotel.

How did the wallet get to the guest house? Most logically, I think, Doctor Sheppard brought it back himself, from wherever he had been. Or he left it there when he went out early that morning.

Once the body was found, once Detective Dillmann came on the case, he went to Florida. He sees the doctor's diary. They won't let us look at the diary, and I don't know why they won't give it to us. But in the diary he sees that Smith was a friend of the doctor's. So he comes back; he gets information from a confidential informer. There's a ten thousand dollar reward hanging around the city. He goes to the Marais Street apartment of John Smith. He sees blood. There's no question there was a lot of blood in the Marais Street apartment on March 3, 1978. The evidence is conclusive, however, that Mr. Smith had vacated those premises on February 4th. Curtis McKnight was living there with all the blood in that apartment. And, Curtis McKnight has vanished. Now, I don't know what Curtis McKnight did in that apartment. I don't know whether he cut up his wife, or whether he got cut. I don't know what happened. But, he flew the coop. He's gone. But, you see, Dillmann had been at the scene with the doctor's body—he had gotten an inventory of all the evidence. He's got a yellow bedsheet. A woman's stocking. A plastic trash bag. Then he's got blood at Marais Street, and he's got Candy Smith. This statement is consistent with the way Dillmann thought this crime occurred. And, that is why we've got that version. Smith told Dillmann what Dillmann wanted to hear. What Dillmann told him to say. He's got the Marais Street apartment in here. He's got the blood in here. He's got the bedsheet in here.

It's unfortunate, and it's a great loss to humanity, that a man with the intelligence, the education, the contribution of Dr. Sheppard is no longer with us. That's terrible. But when a person is lying facedown with a sock stuck down his throat and is strangled, blood is not splattered all over the wall and everything else. It just doesn't happen.

We don't know the blood type. We can't prove, they can't prove, what it was. I looked hard for the doctor's blood type because I know the blood in that apartment was not Doctor Sheppard's blood. Mr. Gee went through the apartment. He didn't see the blood. Daisy went through it. She didn't see the blood. The blood wasn't there. The only person who knows about the blood is Curtis McKnight and he's gone. But, they have in the statement, "blood all over" because that was the way Dillmann figured the case went down.

Now, it is difficult for me to understand why Smith did what he did; why he gave that statement. I would not have done that. Most of you would not have done that. But I don't live that kind of life, and you don't live the kind of life that Smith does. Plus, you probably are not intimidated by police.

What has bothered me a great deal, what I'm very afraid of, what is the sensitive thing in my case, is why John Smith made any statement in the first place. Why did he do that? Why? None of you would do that. Of course you wouldn't. I wouldn't have done it.

You see, in this country, we're supposed to have a trial by peers. Well, John Smith doesn't have a trial by peers. If he had a trial by peers, I'd have an easy job. If he had street people, hustlers, people who have been harassed, people who've been afraid of police, people who've been kicked around, people who tried to survive in a jungle, I wouldn't have any trouble at all. But I do because he doesn't have a trial by his peers. He has a trial by his superiors—people who live differently. None of you would have done that. Of course not. And the prosecutor's going to say, well, convict him because he acted differently from how you would have acted. And, he's going to argue that point eloquently, and logically perhaps, and with some force and persuasion, because he knows the audience that he's talking to. And, he knows that you will have the most difficult time trying to understand why John Smith would make any statement to the police unless he was guilty.

Let me tell you about Dillmann. Dillmann is smooth, very smooth. Dillmann is like those yard lizards sitting out in the sun, putting out their throats, all pretty and green. And you know that no matter how much you want them to change colors, you can't get them to do it. But, when they want to change color, they've got a dark side to them. They can change. You've got to believe that Dillmann—when he testified, and on that tape which he knew the jury was going to hear—had his pretty green side up. But there's a dark side, and that dark side was when they were in that interrogation room, just the two of them, for forty-five minutes before the tape started. And, that's when this story was concocted. That is when this story was concocted.

I told you when we started that before a jury can convict a person, they must be convinced beyond a reasonable doubt and to a moral certainty. I told you that's sufficient. You can't convict on hunches, guesses, suspicions. Now there is a cloud of suspicion over my client. No question about it, because he did what he shouldn't have done: he made a statement. But, only because there is that suspicion, that is not enough to convict. You can't convict on it because we don't know what happened. This doesn't do it. We don't know. There's a suspicion, as far as I'm concerned, on Larry Cephas. He was the last person to see the doctor. There's a suspicion, as far as I'm concerned, on Cabrera, who was in town that weekend, and who was a beneficiary out of a will. There may be a suspicion on others in that last will. I don't know. It's very conceivable. It's possible that when the doctor and Larry Cephas separated that morning at seven-thirty that the doctor went toward the French Market, met a stranger or another sexual encounter, went back to the guest house, and then, before nine or nine-thirty, left suddenly. I don't know what happened. But, it seems to me that the evidence is just as likely that something happened at the guest house as at the Marais Street apartment.

What precisely do they want you to believe? Do they want you to believe that Smith was there, and Patin and Blanks killed the doctor? Now, if that's what they believe, why don't they prosecute Patin and Blanks? They've got the same evidence against them as they have in this case. Why don't they prosecute them? Do they believe, "No, it wasn't Patin and Blanks, it was two other people"? Is that what they believe? Or that Smith did it by himself, that Patin and Blanks really in fact weren't there. They don't know. I don't know. You don't know. The case has not been solved.

Let me remind you of this. It's not a jury's function to solve cases. You may suspect that Smith had something to do with it, but you're not crime solvers. That's not your function. The police and the district attorney have to do that, not you. And that's what they're really asking you to do in this case, just to believe, speculate that it happened this way. But there's no evidence. In fact, all of the evidence indicates it did not happen that way.

You jurors have to understand that as citizens all of us are concerned about the crime rate. All of us are concerned about sending criminals away. You have to realize, however, that now that you're selected to serve on a jury, you're not only a citizen anymore, but a public officer. You have taken an oath, an officer's oath, that you will serve as a juror. And jurors who acquit a person do their duty to society as much as when they convict somebody, when there is sufficient evidence to satisfy them to a moral certainty and beyond a reasonable doubt.

When the State fails in putting forth sufficient evidence to satisfy you beyond a reasonable doubt and to a moral certainty, then you do your duty as a citizen to find that individual not guilty. That's the way the system has to work. The message then goes to the officials, the DA, the police department, the public officials, that they need more money for policemen; that they need better trained policemen; that they need better equipment; that we are not going to simply put people in a cage for life just on hunches and suspicions.

And that is all they have in this case. They have a statement which they themselves don't really believe in. They think he's involved. They have a hunch. They have a suspicion. And they want you to have that hunch and that suspicion. They want you to find him guilty, but without any evidence. There is no evidence at all.

What evidence do they have to corroborate this man? None. None!

All the evidence indicates the crime didn't happen the way it's related in the statement. A person strangled with a sock in his mouth doesn't spurt out blood. But, Dillmann knew there was blood there, so he had to work it into the scene.

When you get right down to it, they want you to take this statement and make a leap in the dark. They want you to jump to a conclusion without any evidence. *They don't have the evidence.*

Now, Smith said, and I asked him, "Why did you give the statement? Why did you do this?" He said he gambled. He gambled that if he gave them a false statement, ultimately he would be vindicated. He said, "I made up Patin and Wendell Blanks." He said, "I knew what would happen. They'd go and arrest them and they would be released, just because they weren't involved," just as he wasn't involved.

Or was he involved? Did he do it by himself? Were there two other people? We don't know. We just don't know.

You would violate your oath and duty as a juror if you convicted this man on a suspicion and on a hunch.

Thank you.

Buddy Lemann's passionate plea left his face drenched in sweat, and his small audience—not many spectators turned out for this third go-round—numb in silence. Had they applauded, which would have been appropriate in another setting, he probably would have taken a bow.

I don't know if anyone could have saved the day. Bob Myers tried. He pointed out:

1) Lemann had turned the felony murder law on its ear. The jury had only Candy's word that the gun used was a toy, and those six years Harold Patin spent in Angola for armed robbery hadn't been for using a toy. Besides, *accessory after the fact of murder* (he admitted helping take the body to Almonaster) *was a felony.* Also, they *intended* to commit a felony. Even if the jury accepted Candy's word that only forty dollars got taken, the killers *expected* to get much more. Most important, regardless of what Candy thought the "others" intended, it was reasonable to assume the result might be homicide, and that's what happened.
2) *No* corroborative evidence, Buddy Lemann said. That confession was a treasure trove of corroboration.
3) Buddy Lemann said there was no motive. How about robbery? How about jealousy? It simply wasn't true that Candy could "get anything he wanted" from Dr. Sheppard. Sheppard's longtime modus operandi had been to give small amounts of money to petitioners.
4) The doctor's wallet. I knew after the first time I talked with Heath and Melerine that it had been found at the Ursulines Guest House. No wallet was located at the dump scene. Candy *said* he

removed the forty dollars from a wallet, but I believe it was from the doctor's pants.

5) McKnight "cut up his wife," Buddy speculated. I saw no sign that she had been cut up, or in any way abused. Lemann's theory was simply ludicrous. The confession made it crystal clear how the blood got on the floor.

6) Smith said "what Dillmann wanted to hear." The record of my time that I so carefully had documented by others didn't allow for this kind of tutoring. And I *couldn't* have coached him about the radio because I didn't know of its existence.

7) Buddy said there was too much blood. He knew better than that, and so did the jury. "Trauma to the right temple," Dr. McGarry wrote in the autopsy report, and testified in court. Sheppard *bled profusely from his right ear,* and also quite possibly from the throat.

8) Why did Smith make this statement? Buddy asked again and again. Simple: He thought he could put the blame on someone else. But even if Buddy wanted to believe his client, then it was because Smith's "conscience" bothered him.

9) The crime "could just as likely" have been committed at the guest house, the lawyer contended. Nonsense, except it made very good sense to get a jury thinking about a hundred different scenarios.

10) Why weren't Patin and Blanks on trial? Lemann knew exactly why, and why we couldn't say.

11) Maybe Cephas did it. Or Cabrera. Or someone else mentioned in the will. Hell, maybe Sheppard's father came back from the grave. The fact is, I'm firmly convinced, John Smith and Harold

> Patin did it, and the book should have been closed.

But jurors make these decisions. By a 10-2 vote, they acquitted John E. "Candy" Smith.

I saw Buddy hand Candy some money out in the corridor. After this fortunate man had hurried down the hallway, I asked Lemann what it had been all about.

"Ah, it was nothing," Buddy said. "That was for bus fare. I told John to get out of town. Go to some nowhere place. Maybe Yazoo City. I advised him, and you know this is true, he has no future in New Orleans."

# • EPILOGUE •

MURDER cases, like politics, can make strange bedfellows. In 1988, after I had retired from NOPD and opened up my own investigative agency, I joined with Buddy Lemann to prove the innocence of a police officer wrongly convicted of murder. This defendant wasn't guilty, I told myself, and proceeded to prove the point, but the irony wasn't lost on me, working "the other side of the fence," that I loved having such an able ally.

Lemann remains one of the premier lawyers in the South. He stands on a very short list whenever some prominent accused anticipates the need for Grade-A legal talent. He no longer teaches at Loyola, however, and the Law Clinic he headed disappeared beneath a wave of budget cuts.

I talked with Buddy over drinks in April 1990, to obtain his perspective on the Candy Smith case. He turned on a cat-that-swallowed-the-canary smile, and maintained that Smith was innocent and justice prevailed.

I looked at him blankly. He sipped his drink.

Bad memories crowded out the much more numerous good ones, and I told Lemann I didn't appreciate him and his ilk painting detectives as sadists and torturers.

"Ahhh," he said, disappointment on his face. Hadn't I yet matured enough to understand the "game"?

A Criminal Court judge sat at the same table. He didn't know about my career, nor did a compelling reason exist why he should. But he didn't think I understood how things worked, either. "How many homicides of yours went to trial?" he asked.

"Two hundred," I said, "give or take a couple."

This amounted to many more murders than he would ever handle. The judge looked disappointed that he couldn't explain the "game" to me.

I kept pressing Buddy Lemann for his analysis of why John Smith got off. The lawyer bobbed and weaved, ducked, acted coy. Then he told me a story.

Daisy Scott, Candy's girlfriend, had phoned Buddy six months after the acquittal: Candy was in trouble again, caught driving a stolen car. Would Lemann please represent him?

"John told me he didn't know how to drive," Buddy said to Daisy.

"He was just saying that," Daisy replied.

Buddy refused to handle the case.

"Talk to Joe Meyer about that stolen car," Lemann said to me. "He can answer your question about why Candy got off better than I can."

I did talk to Meyer. He too had established a successful private practice. I asked him if he remembered the John Smith case.

"Remember?" he said. "For as long as I live!"

"Buddy said to ask you about a stolen car."

"Yeah. I handled that case."

He said it would explain why Smith beat the murder rap."

"Buddy's right."

It turned out that Joe Meyer, the super prosecutor who only handled heaters, personally went after Candy Smith on the comparatively minor stolen car charges. Meyer considered Smith a menace, a murderer, and if he could put him away for a long time for vehicular theft, that was only justice.

Meyer "multiple billed" Candy. He intended to use Smith's prior arrest record from Pensacola, Florida, to establish a career criminal pattern that would allow the judge to impose a very stiff sentence.

The former prosecutor came to this part of the story and simply stopped.

"What happened?" I pressed. "Sounds like you had a winning case."

"Remember that flood in Florida?"

"Vaguely. In 1980, right? Was that Pensacola?" I anticipated a punchline.

"Well," Meyer said, "a few police files were destroyed. Guess whose files were among them."

"Candy's."

"Bingo! And that not only explains why he got a wristslap for the stolen car, but how he walked on the murder beef."

I waited for Meyer to say it, and I can still hear his sad voice: "John Smith is the luckiest son of a bitch who ever lived."

After his acquittal, besides the stolen car, Smith got busted for:

- Simple burglary: three counts of theft; receiving stolen property—he pled guilty and received four years.
- Simple battery—this just eighteen months after receiving "four years."

- Criminal trespass.
- Possession of narcotics, two counts.
- Possession of narcotics, two counts.

Except for the four-year sentence he got for burglary, Smith served no time on the other charges. They were dropped for "insufficient evidence."

Harold Patin, as I would have expected, eclipsed Candy in the getting-arrested department:

- Simple battery.
- Simple battery.
- Simple battery and criminal trespass.
- Disturbing the peace.
- Driving under the influence.
- Public drunkenness, simple battery, and resisting arrest.
- Aggravated battery (using something other than his fists), two counts of felony theft, simple burglary, and receiving stolen property—he received "three years" on these charges, but was out thirteen months later to be arrested for . . .
- Criminal trespass.
- Criminal trespass.
- Possession of narcotics (an opium derivative).
- Disturbing the peace and resisting arrest.
- Criminal trespass and criminal damage to property.

Except for the three-year sentence he got for burglary and a simple battery charge that was dropped by the victim, Patin either pled guilty to the other charges and received no sentence or the charges are still pending.

I saw John Smith once after his acquittal. It was just two months after the jury set him free. I still had nightmares about the case, and the "meeting" was so strange, so bizarre, I sometimes think *I* was lucky the way it worked out.

It was 4:00 A.M., a muggy morning, as I tooled along Orleans Avenue in the plainclothes car. Suddenly a black man made a quick exit from a bar, sprinting into the street.

I recognized him immediately. It was Candy. He evidently hadn't used Buddy Lemann's money for that bus ticket out of town.

Smith froze, lined up like a bull's-eye in my headlights. I can still marvel at the montage of images: Sheppard's bloated body, Candy spilling his guts at Headquarters, the judge twice announcing a hung jury, Smith walking out of lockup, his vindication, and now, yes—Jesus, where did this thought come from?—the punishment and annihilation of a man I knew to be a murderer. The car sped on toward the paralyzed Smith.

In that frozen moment, Smith recognized me. What must have gone through *his* mind?

I ground the car to a halt only a few feet from the petrified man. We locked each other in a long stare before he darted away into the darkness.